Practical Supervision

of related interest

Best Practice in Professional Supervision
A Guide for the Helping Professions
Allyson Davys and Liz Beddoe
ISBN 978 1 84310 995 2
eISBN 978 0 85700 384 3

Mastering Social Work Supervision
Jane Wonnacott
Part of the Mastering Social Work Skills series
ISBN 978 1 84905 177 4
eISBN 978 0 85700 403 1

Passionate Supervision
Edited by Robin Shohet
ISBN 978 1 84310 556 5
eISBN 978 1 84642 749 7

Supervision as Transformation
A Passion for Learning
Edited by Robin Shohet
ISBN 978 1 84905 200 9
eISBN 978 0 85700 509 0

Once Upon a Group
A Guide to Running and Participating in Successful Groups
2nd edition
Maggie Kindred and Michael Kindred
ISBN 978 1 84905 166 8
eISBN 978 0 85700 380 5

Mindful Co-working
Be Confident, Happy and Productive in Your Working Relationships
Clark Baim
ISBN 978 1 84905 413 3
eISBN 978 0 85700 803 9

Inspiring Creative Supervision
Caroline Schuck and Jane Wood
ISBN 978 1 84905 079 1
eISBN 978 0 85700 271 6

Penny Henderson,
Jim Holloway and
Anthea Millar

Foreword by Brigid Proctor
and Francesca Inskipp

Practical Supervision

How to Become a Supervisor for the Helping Professions

Jessica Kingsley *Publishers*
London and Philadelphia

Permission for the cover image has been kindly granted by
Alice Darkling, www.alicedarkling.blogspot.co.uk

First published in 2014
by Jessica Kingsley Publishers
73 Collier Street
London N1 9BE, UK
and
400 Market Street, Suite 400
Philadelphia, PA 19106, USA

www.jkp.com

Library of Congress Cataloging in Publication Data
A CIP catalog record for this book is available from the Library of Congress

British Library Cataloguing in Publication Data
A CIP catalogue record for this book is available from the British Library

ISBN 9781849054423
eISBN 9780857009180

Printed and bound in Great Britain

Contents

Foreword

We were recently asked to offer some training in conjunction with researchers who do extensive organisational research into the effectiveness of clinical supervision. They asked, 'Hasn't anyone done a compact and comprehensive manual on supervision?'

This slim volume is not exactly a manual, but it is compact and comprehensive. We would have been very pleased to refer the researchers to it, had it been published at the time. The authors are steeped in the practice of supervision, the training of supervisors, reading and writing about supervision, and reflecting on their everyday working practice.

Professionals who have shared a preoccupation with consultative or clinical supervision know how much hard work and commitment it takes to:

- distil received wisdom (and sometimes, no doubt, reject nonsense)

- practise in the light of what they hold as valuable theories

- reflect constantly on their own practice

- develop and create their own hypotheses

7

- formulate their changing distillations
- prioritise what to pass on to others.

It is still harder to do that with a minimum of jargon, and to keep it short, focused and thorough. As experienced colleagues, we found new gems and many timely reminders in the pages of this book. It will serve as a very useful and accessible reference source for practitioners at all stages of development. For beginners, it lays out clearly the scope of the many areas which need to be considered when starting to supervise. Throughout, it stresses supervision as a potentially rich aid for developing abilities to reflect *on* practice and *while* practising. It also flags up the temptations that may cause a supervisor or supervisee to forget that active reflection is the prime purpose of the supervisory partnership. In short, *Practical Supervision* will help us all to grow into the truly reflective practitioners we are urged to be and wish to become.

Brigid Proctor and Francesca Inskipp, Fellows British Association for Counselling and Psychotherapy

Acknowledgements

We thank Michael Carroll, Karen John, Brigid Proctor, Francesca Inskipp, Carol Holloway and David Quinton for their critical suggestions and generous encouragement. A special mention is also due to all our supervisees and course participants, who have never failed to inspire us to keep on learning the craft of supervision.

To provide practical case examples in this book, we have drawn on our personal caselore and collective experience as supervisors over many years. All names and details have been changed to protect confidentiality.

Preface

Supervision is first and foremost a process that is *practised.*
From a sound base of theoretical, psychological and ethical
understanding, this practical aspect is at the heart of our
approach at Cambridge Supervision Training where we
work together as trainers. Collaborating with each other
to write *Practical Supervision* has deepened even further our
commitment to developing the reflective practice of both
supervisees and supervisors in many fields.

There are numerous excellent supervision titles, and
many of the best are cited in this book. Our aim is not to
compete with these titles, but to offer a concise, thorough
and resourceful introduction for beginning supervisors in
the helping professions: social and health care, early years
services, psychology, coaching and therapies of all kinds.

We emphasise the importance of a contractual base for
all supervisory practice. Relationship styles in supervision
need to be compatible, so you will be alerted to the
importance of respect for differences that could otherwise
undermine an open, healthy, trusting relationship.
Established models of the tasks and skills of supervision are
presented, along with guidance on shaping sessions and
using authority. We focus on the nuts and bolts of offering
effective feedback to enable all parties in the relationship
to work at their developmental best, and we give particular
attention to supervising and appraising trainees.

Practical ideas for using creative methods and
working with unconscious processes are suggested. We

also introduce group supervision, discuss the essential role played by supervision of supervision, and describe the use of communications technology. While there is a separate chapter on ethics in practice, we take an ethically minded view of all aspects of the supervisory role throughout the book.

Although we draw on diverse resources, our main approach rests on Humanistic and Adlerian ideas and values, focusing on awareness of interpersonal relating, the importance of empathy, equality, and co-operation, and the central need for, and specific skills of, encouragement.

In every chapter of *Practical Supervision* we have used an interactive style and provided short exercises, many drawn from our own training courses, as a means of encouraging you to play an active role in your learning and further develop your reflective skills. Most importantly, we hope that this book will act as a springboard for your continuing interest and increasing pleasure in working as a supervisor.

CHAPTER 1

Introduction
Starting with Yourself

Key points
- Being explicit about your definition of supervision is useful.
- Reflection on your knowledge, skills and values enables choices.
- Essentials of supervision include tasks, relationships and an ethical base.

"'Imagine you are on your way to your supervision session, and think about all the things you don't want to talk about…" said Dave Mearns, Professor at Strathclyde University, at a supervision training session. Plenty of ideas came into our minds, such as when we overran our sessions, the times we found we were talking about ourselves, clients who bored us or made us feel uncomfortable and the times we felt out of our depth. There were sessions where everything was going swimmingly and there just was not anything to say. Dave waited for us to scribble down our thoughts, and then he said very seriously, "…and these are the things you *need* to take to supervision"' (Battye and Gilchrist 2009, p.197).

The purpose of this book is to orient people new to supervision in various helping professions to possibilities and practicalities, and to point readers to useful resources.

Supervision is not the same as management, nor is it like direct work with clients, patients or service users. It requires different frames of thought and some new skills. It is consultative, exploratory and essentially non-judgemental, not ordinarily a time to declare what the supervisee *must* do. It is a boundaried, purposeful relationship with time limits and defined tasks and responsibilities, which means it is not a friendship. Nevertheless, it is most enabling when all parties relax, enjoy being together and feel free to be fully themselves, whether articulating embarrassing or awkward matters or straightforwardly exchanging information. It is designed to support and enable reflective practice. In ideal circumstances it is a place to 'play', in the best sense, and loosen knotted thinking and tangled emotions.

Reflective practice entails using a safely constructed space to develop alternative perspectives about problems. In supervision it is primarily a confidential space where messy emotions provoked by the supervisee's work or affecting their performance can be reviewed, contextualised and released. Developmental issues can emerge, and plans can be made to increase knowledge, skills or emotional awareness in order to cope better with the work.

In many professional contexts supervision is experienced as inspection, control or 'telling off', and thus is seen as a process to be resisted and avoided. We do not see supervision as parental, critical and diminishing. We hold another view of its potential and devote much of this book to describing how to set up and build a relationship that will maximise the sense of the safe space where reflection and learning can flourish.

This time for reflection is hard to carve out in busy workplaces, but it is now well established in therapeutic settings as well as some medical and educational settings.

Without reflection, staff are much more at risk of burnout – the cynical hardening of the human heart.

Many people learn supervision, as they do other helping roles, primarily by observation or unstructured apprenticeship, and doing what someone they admire does in similar circumstances. If your model was good, you may have found yourself imitating your supervisor, rather than developing your own style. If you have had a bad experience, you may be inclined to do the opposite, perhaps being over-influenced by that negative role model. Studying this book, and taking some formal training in supervision, could strengthen your professional confidence in the role and help you to make choices about how to be *yourself* as a supervisor.

CASE STUDY: SUPERVISION ENABLES INSIGHT

George was beside himself with fury. He had just been in a meeting with a colleague who frequently took credit for his own ideas, and this man had done it again. George felt used, invisible, sidelined and powerless. 'I could have been another chair in the room,' he almost shouted, 'not a senior colleague.' By looking with his supervisor at what had happened, George noted his own responsibility for not standing up to the 'ideas thief' and also recognised that there were systemic matters being played out. Their manager deliberately set one against the other, thinking this provoked competitive working. The organisational culture was rigid. Leadership was poor. George was an original thinker in an organisation where routine was important. By the end of the hour with his supervisor, George had a lot of food for thought about his own behaviour and whether he fitted in the organisation. He had been heard, supported and challenged to move from blame to problem solving. New perspectives at the systemic, interpersonal and internal levels had emerged. He felt able to think clearly about things again.

Questions related to supervision

What does supervision mean to you?

Your particular role and the context in which you are working will naturally affect your view of supervision.

> **Reflection point**
>
> Think about the supervision you have received, good and bad. What have you learned from being supervised? How can that guide you to become the supervisor you might want to be?

Why define supervision?

The word 'supervision' has oppressive connotations to some people, so let us be clear that we emphasise the value of equal respect between supervisor and supervisee.

Supervision demands a balance between three very different tasks:

1. To support and encourage people engaged in emotionally demanding tasks.

2. To make sure they know how to do what is expected.

3. To uphold agreed standards and support the supervisee to work towards them.

These tasks require the supervisor to form a respectful and robust relationship with the people they are supervising.

The following are the definitive essentials of supervision for professionals who work in helping roles:

- A working agreement or 'contract', carefully negotiated between supervisor and supervisee(s), is the essential building block for the relationship (see Chapter 2).

- A supervisory relationship must develop mutual trust to be a safe working space. This trust results from shared experiences and direct, honest communication, including respectful challenge (see Chapter 6).

- Talking about personal and professional values and ethics in relation to the work that is being supervised increases understanding of any differences in approach.

If you want someone else's definition, we like this one:

Supervision is a co-operative, facilitating process with a twofold aim. The first is to enable the student or worker 'being supervised' to develop as an effective working person. The second, related aim is to offer a forum in which the worker renders an account of herself in order to assure herself, and anyone else who may be requiring her to be accountable, that she is practising responsibly.

(Francesca Inskipp and Brigid Proctor, personal communication)

Why do you want to be a supervisor?

Perhaps it is part of your job description, or you have independently decided it is a role you want to take. You may have had good experiences as a supervisee or simply see it as the route to career development.

Reflection point
Picture yourself supervising. What do you see that really motivates you to take on the role? Make a list of things you might enjoy about it.

People describe themselves as experienced enough, or ready for the challenge. Some people avoid the role for years because of fear of using or abusing power, or of being disliked.

What knowledge do you want to apply?

A supervisor will normally hold back from giving direct advice or instruction, so that the supervisee can develop confidence and competence in their own style. A supervisor's knowledge includes a grasp of the supervisee's work tasks and context. There are models of supervision, both how to structure a session and how to decide where to focus. These models on shaping a supervision session are described in Chapter 5. The administrative tasks of setting up and sustaining supervision include making the contract for the work, keeping appropriate notes and reports, sustaining arrangements and sorting out money matters (see Chapters 2, 7 and 10).

> *Reflection point*
> Ask yourself: 'What information or experience do I feel able
> to base my supervision work upon?'

What skills do you need?

Essential listening skills for supervisors are largely transferable from people-based practice. Empathic responding and focused questioning are routine, too; however, most new supervisors develop additional skills in summarising and giving feedback, along with the confidence to manage a session and set a climate for safety around disclosing difficulties in the work. Here is an example:

> *Supervisee*: I am afraid of this angry father. He comes in and rants at staff. He intimidates me. What should I do?

> *Supervisor*: You and the team sound really affected by him, feeling scared and so unsafe.

There are many choices about where to focus, such as 'What have you tried so far?' or 'What have you seen colleagues do that works for this man?' or 'Does he get what he wants when he asks calmly?'

Sometimes the supervisee will be reluctant to explore their work or the personal implications of it, and may be dishonest, disingenuous or 'economical' with the truth about their practice. So you do need a detective's ear. It is also important that you train your supervisees in the skills of preparation for supervision so they can build their 'internal supervisor' – their habits of self-supervision and personal awareness. They need to reflect about their own practice regularly, take feedback and increase self-awareness as it applies to their work (Carroll and Gilbert 2011).

What attitudes and values do you want to express?

The value base of this book is derived largely from Adlerian ideas (Ansbacher and Ansbacher 1964). These ideas are now extensively shared by 'strengths-based' approaches (Edwards 2012), which expect the supervisor to respect and value, notice and appreciate the ability and potential of their supervisees. As most management texts now agree, people perform best when they feel appreciated, understood, encouraged and accepted – 'warts and all'. But almost everyone feels shame when they have made mistakes. The supervisory relationship has to make learning from mistakes, coping with uncertainty and processing human emotions a valued, normal, developmental activity. Our supervisees will share their mistakes and vulnerabilities if we as supervisors take risks to speak directly and honestly, and not put ourselves on a pedestal. Yet the role also carries authority, and so we have to discover a way to be authoritative without being authoritarian.

It is very important for all supervisors to know and use the ethical framework within which their supervisees operate. This entails explicit discussion, in early supervision sessions, about values and attitudes to any contentious issues, and especially to issues about difference between supervisee and supervisor (see Chapters 2, 3, 12 and 14).

> **Reflection point**
> What are the most important personal and professional values you would want to hold and express as a supervisor? How might a supervisee recognise these?

Whom do you want to supervise?

You may feel that you wish to share the particular expertise you have acquired from your experience of working in specific roles and places. Some supervisors are keen to work with people of a certain age, gender, sexual orientation, ethnicity or class, either to encourage those like themselves to progress or to give a helping hand to those they see as disadvantaged. Some have no choice as supervisees are allocated to them.

In many work contexts, you might begin to supervise out of necessity because trainees or new recruits require guidance and support. You need to help individuals to understand the nuts and bolts of their new job and how to start working in the specific setting for which they are being trained. If you like an educational role, this may be where you want to work. Supervising within peer groups (see Chapter 13) for mutual support and challenge can be a good way to begin. This helps to gain initial confidence in offering some supervisory interventions.

In some settings you may be expected to offer supervision to colleagues from other disciplines in the team, even if you are younger and less experienced than they are. Offering consultative supervision to others when you have never been trained for the specifics of *their* work requires clarity about the purpose and limits of the supervision, and especially about the limits to your knowledge.

Reflection point

You may want to consider the implications for the relationship of (a) being able to choose your supervisee, or (b) having them allocated, when neither of you feels a free choice has been made. (See Chapters 3, 6, 9, 12 and 14 on power in the relationship.)

How do you see yourself as a supervisor?

Simply being there and willing to listen actively to what your supervisees need to unload will enable them to see and hear themselves more clearly. Then they can work out what they need to do or how they need to be next time they go into work. The supervisor provides another set of eyes, ears, kinaesthetic responses and understanding, and through these channels, offers a new perspective on what is troubling the supervisee. Prior relevant experience from meeting similar situations may give the supervisor other clues and insights. So you may see yourself as a buffer and shock absorber, a guide, a mirror, a teacher, a wise elder, an assessor or a provider of refuge. One psychiatrist described her supervisor as her 'second' in the boxing ring who 'provides refreshment, dries me down with a towel, provides me with a bucket to spit into and gives me vital words of support and encouragement' (Freeth 2004, p.262). It is a humane relationship, ideally designed to be mutually enjoyable and developmental. It may begin with elements of 'pupil-teacher' but needs to develop into mutual learning where the focus is always to consider the needs of those absent people whom the supervisee is serving.

Recommended reading

Woskett, V. (1999) *The Therapeutic Use of Self: Counselling Practice, Research and Supervision.* London: Routledge.

> Chapter 9 (pp.209-28) in this compassionate book encourages readers to reflect on how they use their responses as counsellors or supervisors to gain insight and explore issues in the service of the client.

CHAPTER 2

Beginning Supervision

Key points
- A collaborative and equal relationship underpins productive supervision.
- It is essential to co-create a clearly contracted working agreement.
- Our own and our supervisees' core needs and vulnerabilities require attention.

How to begin as a supervisor
The contract and working agreement

Effective supervision is a collaborative process. Despite likely differences in your own and your supervisee's experience, knowledge, perceptions and culture, it is best founded on a relationship of equality. By creating a clear contract with supervisees, you can explore and address the hopes and requirements of both supervisor and supervisee, as well as agency or organisational expectations. This is an engaging way to enable a respectful and equal relationship. It is also important that this is not a 'one off' fixed agreement, but rather a base from which further regular reviews can occur.

What needs to be included in the supervision contract?

Reflection point

Reflect on your experiences of contracting in supervision either as a supervisee or supervisor. Identify the issues that were addressed. Before reading on, create your own list of issues that you believe would be important to discuss, clarify and negotiate with your supervisees as you begin your work together.

Contracting for supervision has two key aspects: the formal or 'explicit' contract, and the psychological or 'implicit' contract (Scaife 2009). There is also the 'mini' contracting that clarifies what needs to be addressed within each session.

The formal or 'explicit' contract

The formal contract is perhaps most familiar to you. Yet, even here, it is not uncommon in supervisory arrangements to leave some key issues unexplored. This can result in confusion and resentment when assumptions are made rather than openly discussed. Some of the explicit contractual issues that are important to address include the following:

- *Organisational arrangements.* When an external agency or organisation is also involved, the policies and procedures of the organisation need to be identified. Check what input is expected from you as the supervisor, and who holds managerial and clinical responsibility for the clients or service users, and for the supervisee's work. Ensu.27 know what requirements there are from ɩ. organisation for insurance, record keeping, reports and evaluation, and of course, clarify how payment will be made.

- *Codes of conduct and ethics.* You will need to discuss the processes, boundaries, and – crucially – the *limits* of confidentiality in relation to your and your supervisees' codes of ethics. What processes will be undertaken should *either* of you have concerns about the other's practice or that of an organisation? How will boundaries be held regarding personal and professional roles, especially if there are dual relationships?

- *General practicalities.* Clarify the following: venue, mode of sessions (i.e. face-to-face or phone/ e-supervision), time and frequency of sessions, method of payment, cancellation procedures, emergency contact, holiday arrangements and plans for the ending of the contract.

- *Structures within the supervision process.* Confirm how many people and what kinds of workload this supervision contract will address, and how you or others will be monitoring these; also check if your supervisee is receiving supervision elsewhere. What expectations do you and the organisation have for your supervisee's presentation of the work, e.g. verbal, use of recordings or written transcripts? What records will be kept by you, and how? How will reviews or appraisals be carried out?

The psychological or 'implicit' contract

The psychological contract in supervision allows many unspoken expectations, as both supervisor and supervisee, to be spelled out and openly explored. The aim is to co-create an enabling space for both of you to undertake the work without unspoken misunderstandings bubbling away beneath the surface. As such, it can have even greater importance for the future supervisory relationship than the more formal contract. We recommend that you pay particular attention to the following points:

- *Expectations.* Ensure you are clear about what you expect of your supervisees, and discuss how your supervisee views your role: Is it as teacher, expert, friend, confessor, dictator, parent (Hawkins and Shohet 2012)? It is also important and very helpful for building the relationship to ask your supervisees about their hopes and images for successful supervision, as well as their fears and anxieties.

- *Developmental stage and training background.* Offer space to talk about your background experience and stage of development as a supervisor and practitioner, and invite your supervisees to share more about their background. How good a 'fit' is it regarding differences in your stages of development, training and theoretical approach? What difficulties might you anticipate there? How would you 'signpost' and deal with these difficulties if they occur? (See Chapter 7 for more details about developmental stages.)

- *Difference.* Maintaining an open forum for discussion of issues of social and cultural differences between yourself and your supervisee is crucial to explore and keep on review.

Social difference

John Burnham (2012) has created a fine mnemonic that can help us remain mindful of the range of differences that need attention: 'Social GGRRAAACCEEESSS': Gender, Geography, Race, Religion, Age, Ability, Appearance, Class, Culture, Ethnicity, Education, Employment, Sexuality, Sexual Orientation and Spirituality.

Reflection point

Think of a specific supervisory relationship. Drawing on the 'Social Graces' list above, notice what stands out for you in terms of both your own identity and your perception of your colleague's identity. What differences between you could be important to discuss further?

- *Learning style:* Check with your supervisees regarding how they learn best, and clarify your preferred facilitating style as a supervisor. Discuss how any possible major differences in learning style might impact on your work together.

Learning styles

Four common learning styles have been identified by Honey and Mumford (1982):

Activists learn best by doing and by plunging into action feet first; *theorists* learn best by first understanding the theory behind the actions; *pragmatists* need to put their learning into practice in the real world; and *reflectors* learn best by first standing back, observing and thinking about the events.

> **Reflection point**
> Think of a recent learning situation. Which of the above styles work best for you? How can you ensure that you meet the needs of a supervisee with a different learning style?

- *Boundaries.* Discuss with your supervisee how boundaries will be kept between supervision of their workload and the supervisee's personal issues. The restorative function (see Chapter 4) is an important part of supervision. This may include your enabling the supervisee to share and explore difficult feelings re-stimulated by the work; however, your contract also needs to clarify that this exploration will keep the work as the primary focus. This means not blurring the boundaries of the relationship by moving *unilaterally* into counselling or other forms of support.

- *Maintaining the working alliance.* Communication of empathy, trustworthiness, authenticity and appropriate use of authority is crucial for developing the contract. This needs to be accompanied by the specific skills of active listening such as reflecting, paraphrasing, summarising, focusing, open and Socratic questioning and immediacy.

> **Reflection point**
> Bring to mind a supervisory experience that has been difficult for you. Reflect on how far these difficulties might have been eased through having a clearer contract.

Contracting for each session

The main contract will provide invaluable containment for the work in each session; however, it will still be important for you to work together to clarify the agenda for each new session, so that no assumptions are made and the needs of your supervisees are freshly accommodated. This is about starting with the end of the session in view and agreeing how you are going to get there together. Some possible open questions to have up your sleeve, either spoken directly or kept in mind, include:

- 'What do you want to focus on?'

- 'What is your key supervisory question?'

- 'How do you want to use your time now?'

- 'What do you most want to achieve in this session and how can we work together best to achieve that?'

At the end of each session, actively invite feedback from your supervisee about the usefulness of the session with questions such as:

- 'What are you taking away with you today?'

- 'What was useful about this session and what was less helpful?'

Paying attention to our human needs

Another starting point in supervision, one which is easily overlooked, is having an understanding of both our own and our supervisees' ordinary human needs and associated vulnerabilities. Alfred Adler stated that 'to be human means to have inferiority feelings' (Adler, as cited in Ansbacher and Ansbacher 1964, p.115). When experiencing the stress of inferiority feelings, and its associated discouragement, we may all be prone to over-compensate for these difficult sensations through some form of 'acting out' response. A helpful framework for understanding our human needs is provided by Lew and Bettner's model of the 'Crucial Cs' (1995). They remind us that we all need to feel that:

- We belong and *Connect.*

- We can take responsibility and feel *Capable.*

- We are significant and can make a difference, and therefore, we *Count.*

- We can handle difficult situations and overcome fear with *Courage.*

These needs are so crucial that if we do not feel they are met in a constructive way, we will find other less useful ways of achieving them; however, as supervisors, by identifying the specific needs being expressed, we can avoid getting into a destructive dynamic and work on positively enabling the missing 'Crucial Cs'.

CASE STUDY: THE MISSING 'CRUCIAL Cs'

Frances, newly employed within a hospital, had attended two supervision sessions with Hasan. Both times she had interrupted him with theoretical references, identifying her extensive reading. Hasan was aware of feeling irritated and of wanting, in turn, to 'show off' his knowledge; however, he also noted to himself that, in her new role, Frances may not have been feeling capable, or feeling that she counted, and hence over-compensating with her 'superiority' in her reading. Hasan then changed tack and acknowledged Frances' theoretical understanding, and he invited her to share more about how she wanted to 'make her mark' in the hospital. Frances visibly relaxed and began to interact less defensively.

Reflection point

Bring to mind two specific occasions as supervisee or supervisor - one when you felt discouraged and one when you felt encouraged. What did you feel and what did you do? See if you can identify (a) which of the 'Crucial Cs' was missing in this situation, and (b) which of the 'Crucial Cs' was being met in your positive experience.

Recommended reading

Hawkins, P. and Shohet, R. (2012) *Supervision in the Helping Professions* (4th ed.). Maidenhead: Open University Press (McGraw-Hill).

Chapter 6 (pp.68–82) provides a useful overview of forming the contract and also explores developmental models.

Scaife, J. (2009) *Supervision in Clinical Practice* (2nd ed.). Hove: Routledge.

Chapter 4 (pp.69–98) offers an excellent and thorough review of the contracting process.

CHAPTER 3

Knowing Your Relationship Style

> **Key points**
> * It is important to be aware of your preferred relationship style.
> * Flexibility in relational style is important.
> * Mutuality enables productive meeting points in supervision.

The essential functions of the supervisory role can be carried out in many styles. There is no single 'correct' way to do effective supervision, but there are specific factors that could influence how you 'get it right' for each of your supervisees so that they feel safe and supported. In particular, the presence of emotionally charged inferiority/superiority dynamics in the relationship makes it crucial to keep alert to how you use your power and authority. This chapter takes a practical look at these relational issues and invites you to think about their impact on your developing style as a supervisor.

Testing your adaptability

Every supervisory relationship is different (which is partly what makes it such stimulating work) – no two supervisees are alike, even if they are employed in identical roles in the same organisation. Some practitioners are ambivalent about going for supervision, perhaps because it involves a kind of 'professional intimacy' which can feel exposing or unsafe. As every individual brings differing 'styles, preferences, passions and aversions' (Proctor 1997, p.190) to their sessions, it is important as a supervisor to be well aware of the following:

Your own preferred relational style

Do you feel most comfortable working with a clear agenda and a tight structure, or is your character better suited to 'creative drifting' in dialogue? Are you a naturally talkative and demonstrably empathic person, or do you prefer to relate from a less verbal and more quietly intuitive place in yourself? Are you habitually cool or warm, lively or still, fast or slow? There is, of course, no 'good' or 'bad' about any of these qualities: the point is to be fully conscious of what you like best and enjoy about yourself as a successful relationship builder.

How you adjust to other styles

How ready or willing are you to make conscious modifications to your preferred mode of relating? Your supervisee might appear to you as a brisk, risk-taking animal, leaping from branch to branch, while you see yourself as a cautious, slow-moving creature, sitting on the ground. How might this difference in 'first nature' get in the way of a trusting relationship, or enhance it? In this example, to assist the growth of a fruitful supervisory alliance you might decide to adapt your style and do a bit of tree-scrambling; or, in discussion with the supervisee, you might both recognise that your steady groundedness is exactly what is needed to support their high-flying work.

The extent of your range

An interpersonal relationship can sometimes stretch you so uncomfortably that it can become painful. Even the most flexible supervisor must be aware of the limits to their stylistic adaptability. When emotional or physical discomfort in relationship with a supervisee is marked, it may need attending to at a deep psychological level, perhaps using the psychodynamics of transference and parallel process (see Chapter 9). To explore the meanings of such unconscious phenomena within the supervisory frame, it is helpful to know your 'default setting' with each supervisee.

Reflection point

In what way do you use your natural temperament to help form professional relationships? What might be the advantages and disadvantages of having a range of relational styles as a supervisor?

Building on strengths

As a supervisor, whether you are temperamentally bubbly or dry, sedate or zappy, you will be drawing on a rich resource of life experience and personal attributes to enable yourself to do the work with a positive attitude. Many of the finely honed strengths you use in relationship building will be evident in the supervisee, too, and a robust working alliance can be founded on these shared qualities.

This approach intentionally sidesteps a 'deficit model' of supervising. Recognise and affirm your supervisee's skills and assets first, then notice what resources might be missing or need improvement. Having identified the strengths a supervisee brings to their role, what is a practical way of regularly letting them know what you have seen? Our primary feedback tool is, of course, the language we use.

'Very good! You did much better than I expected. You're really quite skilful. The way the situation went was quite something. Fantastic stuff – keep up the good work!'

What would you feel in response to hearing these words from someone supervising you? Would you feel pleased, flattered, amazed – or perhaps mistrustful, confused, annoyed? The language above is typical of *praise*, which is usually evaluative ('very good'), comparative ('better than expected') and superlative ('fantastic'). Despite its well-intentioned upbeat tone, praise fails to identify any specific strengths; in fact, on closer inspection, you might agree it has almost no content!

Now let us examine a different kind of feedback:

'You stuck with this unreliable client and were able to put aside your frustration and continued to offer your time and attention. You rehearsed speaking tactfully to her and found a way to connect. I saw your patience being sorely tested, and you persevered.'

This feedback employs several descriptive *verbs* identifying what the supervisee has actually done ('stuck with… put aside…continued…rehearsed...' etc.) without any unnecessary evaluation or comparison. Adding a hearty 'Bravo!' at the end would then have real meaning for the supervisee, since they have been given clear statements about *what they did,* and not vague remarks about *how they were doing.* This is one key to offering encouragement in feedback, which is explored in more detail in Chapter 6, and you will find many other examples throughout this book.

> *Reflection point*
> What is the predominant style of your own (past and present) supervisors? How much have you had to adapt to their style? What is it that they say or do which genuinely encourages you?

Meeting in the middle

How your style as a supervisor affects the inevitable asymmetry of power in the supervisory relationship needs close attention. Is taking your authority and acting powerfully second nature to you? Are you willing but not accustomed to making strongly authoritative interventions? Perhaps you are extremely concerned never to act oppressively? Whatever your stance, it is always helpful to consider the supervisee's possible feelings of powerlessness or inferiority in relationship with you.

A model that offers a very useful conceptual view of this inter- and intrapersonal dynamic (Sweeney 2009) has been nicknamed the slippery pole. The metaphor suggests that 'swooshing up' to take a somehow superior relational position is a subjective movement many people make when they experience a 'felt sense' of inferiority. This inevitably creates 'slippage' in the relationship.

The slippery pole image reminds us that useful connection and authentic co-operation are more likely to happen when people, even with their differences in experience and expertise, can meet as individuals of equal worth. This productive meeting point in supervision can be reached more easily when the interpersonal style of the senior or 'superior' partner is conducive to an atmosphere of mutuality. What would be your impression of a supervisor who behaved as if they had never made any errors in judgement and knew all the answers to everything? Such a person is likely to come across as aloof and intimidating – authoritarian rather than authoritative – and be met with 'spurious compliance' in response.

Reflection point

To what extent can a supervisory relationship be one between equals? Does your personal style lend itself well to an egalitarian approach to supervising?

Recommended reading

Henderson, P. (2009) *A Different Wisdom: Reflections on Supervision.* London: Karnac Books.

Chapter 3 ('Relationship Climates') discusses 'cool' and 'warm' emotional styles in supervision and explores how these can affect the working relationship.

Millar, A. (2007) 'Encouragement and other Es.' *Therapy Today 18,* 2, 40–42.

This article describes how encouragement is an essential ingredient for supervision.

CHAPTER 4

Attending to Tasks and Skills

Key points
- The normative task addresses standards.
- The restorative task combines creativity and self-care.
- The formative task supports the professional development of the supervisee.

Broadly, you aim for a balance between supporting a good standard of work by the supervisee and enabling their professional development by attending to *normative, formative* and *restorative* tasks. All supervisors must manage the administrative tasks related to any work in an organisation, and especially to responsibilities and conflicts that arise between, for example, a training organisation and a placement. Some workplaces and theoretical approaches give more emphasis to standard setting or educational tasks than others. Significant attention to self-development as a professional is essential for creative and resilient work.

CASE STUDY: BEING RESPONSIVE
ABOUT DEVELOPMENT
_____

Joe has just been promoted to nursery manager and has a supervisory role. The workplace is stressful, but people are not expected to complain. He begins a supervision session by discussing courses which a shy and unconfident staff member might attend, and is taken aback when she begins to cry. She reveals that she hates going on courses but is keen to progress. After further exploration, they decide she can follow a structured work-based programme, and he will mentor her through regular monthly supervision meetings.

Definitions of supervisory tasks

Inskipp and Proctor (1988, 1993) chose this memorable trio of rhyming names for these essential tasks: normative, formative and restorative.

Normative tasks

The supervisory contract and the work need to be based on clearly identified answers to the following questions about responsibilities and standards:

- Who manages the practitioner?

- What confidentiality or feedback is expected?

- What evaluation and monitoring of the work is required?

- Who will have access to the practitioner's notes, and indeed, the supervisor's notes?

- What standards are expected? (It is crucial that expectations be explicit when working with trainees.)

- Is there a complaint procedure?

- Is the supervisor expected to write a report or take part in appraisals, and if so, who will see any documents about this essentially confidential relationship?

Routine monitoring, even of the number of hours of work being done, and whether the boundaries of the normal professional relationship with clients or patients are being sustained, is important. More extreme issues include:

- Is the practitioner breaching an ethical imperative?

- Are they doing harm?

- Should they get a supervisory report to allow them to pass the course if their work is not quite safe enough?

Supervision also keeps the supervisee alert to the wider context in which they are employed and the implications of agency policies on the work they do.

Formative tasks

Formative tasks refer to the educational tasks of the supervisor, but most of the time it is not purely a 'teaching' task. Supervision invites thoughtful reflection about what works and about mistakes, encouraging supervisees to notice their tacit knowledge and find their own artistry as a practitioner. This promotes learning from practice to integrate experience with theory. Supervisors can choose when to offer to fill in gaps in knowledge by recommending references or demonstrating skills. Most often, supervisors are influential just by their own behaviour during supervision, which, in ideal circumstances, acts as a model for direct and empathic interpersonal communication.

Restorative tasks

Restorative tasks aim to enable the development of the supervisee towards greater self-awareness and professional resilience, but without turning the supervision into therapy or intrusive questioning. Resilience can be noted by a 'check-in' at the beginning of a supervision session to ask how the practitioner is and what is occurring in their life that might affect the work. An example is given below.

Pat (supervisor): How are you?
Supima (supervisee): My grandmother just died, and I am so tired I find it hard to come to work.
Pat: My condolences. She was important to you, wasn't she? What specifically are you finding hard?
Supima: Mrs Grey. She reminds me a lot of my Gran. I just feel sad.
Pat: Are you speaking to someone about this at home?
Supima: Yes, I tell my mum.
Pat: Here, do you feel you can do the work even though you are feeling sad?
Supima: Yes, and I feel better now that you know.

This task is also one that enables creativity when there is enough mutual trust to 'play' with metaphor, imagery or creative resources (see Chapter 8). For instance, we can use the analogy of eagles and frogs. Is the supervisee soaring enough over the territory of their work to see the bigger picture? Or are they like the mythical frog, who can be put into a pot of warm water and allow itself to boil and die if the heat is turned up slowly enough? Sometimes the supervisee may need support to consider leaving a seriously unhealthy working environment for the sake of her or his own well-being.

Reflection point

Reflecting on each of these three tasks, which do you spend the most time on when you are a supervisee? If you were to ask your supervisor to change the balance, what would you like your supervisor to attend to more?

Exercise: Applying the Normative, Formative and Restorative Model

When talking about one of their patients, your supervisee says, 'This teenager is just like my own: silent, shut down, avoiding eye contact. I can't get anywhere with him, but I am worried about his safety.' What would you reply if offering a (a) normative, (b) formative or (c) restorative response? Here are some examples:

Normative responses:
'What are your worries about his safety?'
'What is your knowledge of safeguarding protocols in this agency?'
'Did he choose to come or has he been sent?'
'How confident is he about confidentiality?'

Formative responses:
'What do you know about normal teenage development?'
'What's different here?'
'You say you can't get anywhere with him. What have you been doing together so far?'

Restorative responses:
'Tell me more. How is your teenager the same or different from this one?'
'Are you worried about yours, too?'
'How is it affecting your work with him?'
'You look upset. Is there something that has been happening at home that you want to talk about here?'

Supervisory skills to implement the tasks

Normative skills are those entailed in using authority, such as:

- direct communication that makes clear if a supervisee *must* do something or stop doing it (such as giving out their personal mobile phone number if the organisation forbids this)

- discussion about what a supervisee *may* want to try, or what they *can* do because the practice fits with ethical standards or organisational norms

- assessment skills and giving feedback, which are essential parts of this category.

Formative skills include:

- careful, accurate listening

- Socratic questioning (see Chapter 6) that draws out the supervisee's own wisdom

- timely advice about practicalities such as records to keep or application of theoretical ideas.

Most specifically, the supervisor invites the supervisee to notice *how* they learn as well as *what* they learn.

Restorative skills take two paths. First, the creative skills include:

- clear contracting, so the supervisee does not fear being intruded upon, with the supervision moving into therapy

- applying those skills the supervisee already uses with people, such as working intuitively with imagery, metaphor, drawing or little objects, all of which invite the supervisee to reflect upon their own internal processes or to see an external pattern of relationships more systemically.

Here the supervisee is validated for their intuitive and sensory responses, and these are made coherent and reviewed through reflection.

The second restorative path requires us not to offer therapy, but to:

- enquire about the supervisee's well-being

- encourage the supervisee into greater self-awareness when appropriate to the task

- offer a space for reflection about the interface between work and home, or health and family.

In an early study that explored the value of supervision during counsellor training, Scanlon and Baillie (1994) reported respondents describing their relationship with their supervisor as 'feeling "held", "seen", "heard", "listened to", "validated", "supported", "reinforced" and "valued"' (p.418). These are consequences of good attention to the restorative skills in any professional training.

Monitoring your own work as a supervisor

Take time to think about each relationship with a supervisee and how productive it seems. Ask yourself:

- How do you assess the usefulness of your balance of tasks with each one?

- Is the supervisee developing confidence?

- Can they disagree with you and give reasons why, and still be on good terms with you?

- Do they come prepared and ready to work?

- Have you made explicit any concerns you have about their practice, and if so, what was the consequence for your relationship?

- Do supervisees choose to stay with you, and if so, does this feel healthy or too dependent?

To enable thorough monitoring of your supervision work, it is hugely beneficial to have occasional supervision of supervision, either with a highly experienced supervisor or with a formal group of peers (see Chapters 13 and 14).

Recommended reading

Millar, A. (2009) 'Developing skills: Practice, observation and feedback.' In P. Henderson (ed.) *Supervisor Training: Issues and Approaches*, pp.107-22. London: Karnac Books.

This chapter identifies essential skills and attitudes needed for constructive and encouraging feedback in supervision; see especially the summary of skills on p.113.

CHAPTER 5

Shaping a Supervision Session
Choices of Focus

Key points

- Session structure and time management are mostly the responsibility of the supervisor.
- Choosing where to focus may be based on content or process.
- It is always important to pay attention to the resilience of the supervisee.
- Journals and logs are useful reflective tools.

Every effective supervisor develops habits of shaping supervisory sessions. A minimum structure is the beginning, the working section and the end. Some authors (e.g. Page and Woskett 2001) suggest a sequence like this, whereas others want the supervisor to look through different pairs of spectacles or 'eyes' and choose a focus depending on what is being brought. In actual practice, what are you used to doing?

The beginning period has two tasks: (a) to find out how the supervisee is, and (b) to agree on the goals of the session. Generally, this should take less than ten minutes of an hour's supervision. If the supervisee is in the midst of difficult life events, there is a risk that telling about it, even in relation to work, can spill over to dominate the session. Supervision then can become more like therapy, and the boundary shifts from supporting the work to a space for individual concerns. You can start by linking the two tasks to set the tone and remind the supervisee of the supervisory focus. For example, you could say, 'Tell me how you are and what you want from this session'. If the practitioner cannot focus on the work, you may need to talk with them about their personal resilience and current capacity for working safety and effectively.

The middle period is when the reflective work about clients or workplace issues is undertaken. A useful ending requires both parties to share responsibility to keep some minutes for an end-of-session review. This is difficult. It requires the supervisor to monitor time rigorously.

Most supervisees really want to use the time for work on their clients or patients and organisational concerns. Yet research by West and Clark (2004) revealed that when the supervisor and supervisee were asked immediately after a session what was most useful, it was quite common for them to name different moments and interventions. Supervisees seldom say what the supervisor has done that was *un*helpful, unless the supervisor explicitly asks for this feedback. Useful review questions include:

- 'What have you learned from this session?'
- 'What are the next steps you will take?'
- 'What could be better next time we meet?'
- 'What were the most and least useful parts of today's meeting?'

The shape of a session

In a humane and practical book about supervision, Page and Woskett (2001) suggest that a good supervision session may have five stages: contract, focus, space, bridge and review. Having made your session *contract* and agreed on the *focus*, there is the *space* where the worker is held, supported, challenged and affirmed in their work. 'Supervisory space' is where movement and insight can occur as a result of the exploratory work undertaken by the supervisor and supervisee. It is also a place where 'not knowing' and confusion are accepted and tolerated in the belief that time and attention given to relational or organisational issues and to the supervisee is beneficial, even when a comfortable resolution of issues may not be achieved. This period is followed by the *bridge*, which is for goal setting and planning how to take insights forward, and then the *review*.

Reflection point
What shape of a supervision session has been of most use to you as a supervisee? How do you ask for what you want?

How to choose a focus

A number of authors have suggested ways to focus, but Hawkins and Shohet (2012) have provided the ideas that have come to dominate the UK training of supervisors. They suggest seven modes (later called 'eyes' to emphasise that these are different perspectives). This may feel like too much to hold in mind for new supervisors, who commonly feel overwhelmed. But as the use of the seven eyes becomes more familiar through habit and practice, this model becomes an excellent focusing tool that can be shared with the supervisee and used as a basis for reflection afterwards. Many supervisors discover that they have two or three preferred areas of focus, and through reflection on this they learn to extend their range.

Eye 1 – Content of the supervision session: Picture the person

The supervisor enables the supervisee to focus on the service user they have in mind, and to think about aspects of this person's life that might lead to new insights or more empathic feelings about them. New supervisors habitually focus here.

Eye 2 – Supervisee interventions and responses: What is the supervisee doing?

What the supervisee did and said, why, and what they might do or say next. The supervisor supports the supervisee to explore different ways of working, and may point out habitual ways of intervening and invite the supervisee to notice what is most effective.

Eye 3 – The supervisee/client relationship: How are you getting on?

This entails exploration of the dynamics of the relationship and how it is developing. The reflection about the relationship, and about transferential issues (if this fits with the supervisee's model of working), may reveal feelings of which the supervisee was unaware and provide a space to release them.

Eye 4 - Internal process of the supervisee: How am I being affected by this person?

The supervisee can become more aware of their thoughts, feelings, theories, bodily processes, dreams or fantasies about the client, and thus begin to sort out what belongs to them and what belongs to the client. This supports them to develop increased self-awareness and may create links between their theory and practice.

Eye 5 - The supervisor/supervisee relationship: How are we getting on?

By exploring the supervisory relationship, either person may also become more aware of unconscious messages between supervisee and client. The supervisor aims to explore their own relationship with the supervisee in a non-judgemental way (see the section on parallel process in Chapter 9).

Eye 6 - The supervisor's internal processes: How am I being affected by this supervisee?

Thoughts, feelings or bodily sensations of the supervisor in the session are used and explored as possible clues to how the client or supervisee might be affecting others (see Chapter 9).

Eye 7 - Systems: organisational, cultural, professional, familial, societal, ethical. In which systems are we caught up?

The contexts in which the client, supervisee and supervisor operate can affect the work. Contact times may be limited;

outcomes may be monitored; standards and ethical imperatives may be prescribed. In addition, families or the organisation may demand improved behaviour of the client, or cultural imperatives may forbid some behaviours. Individual or organisational finances may suddenly change. There are very many ways that the system may affect the work significantly. Usually, personal issues interact with systemic pressures, as evidenced in the scenario below.

CASE STUDY: APPLYING THE SEVEN-EYED MODEL

Supervisor Rhiannon and supervisee Ed (who works for a charity running support groups for young carers) are about halfway into a session.

Rhiannon: You began talking excitedly about the new funding coming in next year, and now you look very thoughtful…almost sad.

Ed: Yes… I do feel kind of weighed down. I'm aware how many kids out there are not getting the help they need. It's so frustrating – this huge uncertainty about funding all the time.

Rhiannon: Frustration and uncertainty…that's a heavy combination. I'm starting to feel it, too. What can we do here that might lighten the load a little?

Ed: Moaning helps! But I don't want to use all my supervision time just to moan.

Rhiannon: OK. Let's focus in for five minutes or so. Who is it, confidentially, you would most like to have a good moan about?

Ed: Well…there's a colleague who…she's like a big kid. Fun, but unreliable.

Rhiannon: How concerned are you about her competence in the job?

Ed: Oh, she does the job OK. She just gets away with things.

Rhiannon: I know you are very conscientious about your role and like to follow the rules. Your co-worker seems to take a looser approach.

Ed: Exactly. We're very different. Actually she gets much more playful with the service users than I do.

Rhiannon: When she does that, what are you like with the service users?

Ed: More the responsible parent – which is me all over! I keep a constant eye on everything. It's not playtime for me. I relate to the quiet kids, the shy ones.

Rhiannon: Seeing how well you take care of all the practicalities, I imagine they quickly feel safe with you.

Ed: Yes, I suppose I am like that. Safety is the first thing on my mind.

Rhiannon: What has happened recently that hasn't felt safe?

Ed: One young lad became agitated and started throwing things, causing havoc. I talked to him and it turned out he was secretly scared of his step-mother, who has a drinking problem.

Rhiannon: Sounds like he really opened up to you. How were you able to help him?

Ed: We talked about how he could ask his father to tell her to stay out of his room in the evenings.

Rhiannon: A fine practical suggestion. What happened?

Ed: He told me it caused a row between the parents, but his step-mum did leave him alone.

Reflection point

Identify when the supervisor is using the different 'eyes'. Look especially for the way 'eye seven' allows the supervisor to check that the service is being offered safely.

Keeping a journal

If you want to discover what works best for you as a supervisor, keep detailed notes or start a journal about your supervisory sessions. Journal keeping helps develop positive habits of reflection (Progoff 1975) for both supervisor and supervisee. A journal mirrors the reflective process of supervision and can help the supervisee prepare for it. Some ideas for prompts that the supervisee might use for journal writing are listed below:

- Notice what happens and/or how you feel about it.

- Reflect on the meaning of this.

- Try something new, if necessary.

- Have a safe place to tell the story of what happened.

- Use the attention of another person to help you reflect on it, if it is not obvious.

- Set the next goal or task, or continue to monitor that to which you have agreed.

Scaife (2010, p.214) describes 'learning logs' and reflective diaries in supervision. She notes that they can improve capacities to sustain curiosity, record implications for practice, connect learning that has come from different settings, clarify thinking, express feelings or act as an aide-mémoire.

Supervisors benefit, too. Hawkins and Shohet (2006, p.145) describe a course they offer for experienced supervisors to take on *consultative* supervision and provide the following questions to assist review of a supervision session during training:

- What do you notice the supervisor focusing on? Why do you think they are doing this?

- What do you think the session achieved?

- What strategies did you notice being used by the supervisor?

- What did the supervisor ignore that you might have worked with?

- What did the supervisor work with that you might have ignored?

- What makes them switch from focusing on one process to another? How effective is the switch?

Recommended reading

Hawkins, P. and Shohet, R. (2006) *Supervision in the Helping Professions* (3rd ed.). Maidenhead: Open University Press (McGraw-Hill).

> NB: Their 'seven-eyed model' is summarised on pp.80-103, and pp.140-46 describes their advanced supervisor training course with details about using video effectively and training in transcultural and ethical supervision. (The 4th 2012 edition summarises their model on pp.85-111 but does not include the questions listed above.)

Page, S. and Woskett, V. (2001) *Supervising the Counsellor: A Cyclical Model*. Hove: Brunner-Routledge.

> The authors' five-stage supervision model is described on pp.30-44.

CHAPTER 6

Giving and Getting Feedback

> **Key points**
> - Effective feedback is dependent on a positive supervisory relationship.
> - Feedback is a two-way process creating a meeting point between supervisor and supervisee.
> - Encouragement is at the heart of effective feedback, which involves identifying strengths as well as offering challenge.

Providing enabling feedback and appropriate challenge is a core process in supervision. It supports practitioner competence, strengthens effective workplace management and safeguards client welfare. Equally, being open to feedback from supervisees is a crucial aspect of a positive and sustaining supervisory relationship.

> **Reflection point**
> What are your hopes and fears about giving feedback to supervisees? What is particularly difficult for you when giving feedback? What makes it easier for you to give feedback?

How to create a meeting point with supervisees

Effective feedback is about enabling growth, learning and improved practice. It can be seen as an interaction, or a *meeting point* between you and your supervisees, rather than something that you 'give out' to them. One-sided feedback in supervision invariably creates a power imbalance, even when you share positive comments.

It is very important that your working agreement has clearly identified structures and good understanding about all assessment and feedback processes that will take place between you and your supervisees. This needs to include opportunities for the supervisee to share their experience of supervision. The feedback process then becomes a norm – a valuable, rather than dreaded, part of the supervision.

Core principles for giving feedback

Hawkins and Shohet's (2012) acronym 'CORBS' offers a helpful reminder of the key principles for giving feedback:

Clear: Be clear about what feedback you wish to give.

Owned: Be aware that your feedback is your own perception and not an ultimate truth.

Regular: Give feedback regularly and as close to the event as possible.

Balanced: Ensure a balance between positive and challenging feedback.

Specific: Accompany any feedback with specific detail and description.

Building courage in supervisory work

Central to all effective supervision is feedback that provides *encouragement*. This is different from traditional praise or rewards, as it focuses on enabling both supervisor and supervisee to develop an *inner* sense of satisfaction and motivation. 'En-*courage*-ment', with courage at its heart, involves acknowledging strengths while also offering a supportive framework for challenge as needed. For encouragement to work, supervisors need to create a climate of equality and collegiality with their supervisees, even where there is a difference in experience and expertise. This provides a potent foundation that helps us face our fears and have the 'The Courage to be Imperfect' (Dreikurs 1970).

Encouragement involves much more than expressing positives (Millar 2007). Different from praise, encouragement focuses on *what* the person is doing, rather than *how* the person *compares* with others. Verbal encouragement can be achieved by avoiding the use of adjectival labels such as 'good', 'unethical', 'clever' and 'non-empathic', and by keeping in mind the assets and *intentions* of the supervisee.

By using descriptive language and paying particular attention to *verbs*, you can offer feedback that is very specific, identifying what the supervisee has actually been doing, without needing to evaluate it. For example, an evaluative label such as 'You're hopeless with boundaries and get far too involved with your patients' becomes 'I notice that instead of the allotted half-hour, you regularly stay for one hour with your patient, and that you made an additional home visit out of work hours when it was this patient's birthday'.

> *Reflection point*
> Think of a supervisee or colleague with whom you have concerns and difficulties. Identify any negative labels that come into your mind. Now turn these labels into specific non-evaluative descriptions using verbs as illustrated above. What positive intentions may be behind the actions? (You may wish to refer to the 'Crucial Cs' model described in Chapter 2.)

From this non-attacking base, you can invite the supervisee's own views, and then share any concerns, providing educative information and supportive challenge as appropriate. Here respectful use of 'signposting' is helpful. Just as it is crucial on a motorway to be prepared for a junction a good mile or so before, we can signpost our feedback in advance so it is less startling and enables a more collaborative meeting point. For example: 'I'd like to discuss the ethical issue that may be involved in this situation – can we look at this now?' Further space can then be given for two-way discussion with the supervisee.

CASE STUDY: DESCRIPTIVE FEEDBACK

Shona was supervising Alan's coaching work with B, who had recently come out as gay to his parents. The parents had proved to be very critical and rejecting. Shona had noted Alan's impatience and criticism of B in having 'been so long in coming out' and how 'he should just forget about his parents'. Shona was concerned about Alan's attitude, although she also wondered whether this was an echo of the parents' critical dynamics. Shona responded by describing, rather than reactively labelling, his actions. She then signposted the issues she felt it was important to address, also inviting Alan's feedback on her comments:

'You opened up some valuable exploration with B about his sexuality. Where there seemed to be a loss of connection was in being able to empathise with B's feeling of vulnerability when sharing this with his parents. I have some thoughts about the dynamics that might be going on here, and possibly how this might be worked with in your future coaching sessions, that I would like to discuss with you. What do you think about what I've said?'

The use of Socratic questions can also help supervisees focus more deeply on their work, thus keeping a two-way flow of communication. This type of questioning invites the supervisee to gain insight into their own perceptions and then, ultimately, their own wisdom. For example:

'When you say you find this young person difficult, what specifically do you mean?'

'What do you appreciate about the way you handled that?'

'How might you do things differently in future?'

'What do you plan to take away from our discussion?'

Written feedback

Two-way feedback can still take place in written work. It is about keeping the question 'What is happening?' in mind, describing the interventions and intentions observed. You can then note and share your thoughts on areas that you believe would be important for further development. This helps to create a meeting point between you and your supervisee.

Reflection point

What are your hopes and fears about receiving feedback from your supervisees? What makes it easier for you to receive feedback? What is particularly difficult for you when receiving feedback?

Being able to receive feedback in a constructive way is a skill in itself, and is far from a passive process. Whether in the role of supervisor or supervisee, some form of defensiveness is likely when receiving feedback. Maybe because this triggers old feelings of shame, from which we defend ourselves by shrinking and losing our sense of capability, or perhaps we over-compensate for our feelings of inferiority by becoming aggressive. Either way, this inhibits potential learning and growth. The challenge is to be able to listen openly to the feedback, and identify how, if at all, this might support our future practice.

As described earlier, Hawkins and Shohet (2012) offer the following guidelines linked with their acronym 'CORBS':

- If necessary, ask for the feedback to be more Clear, Owned, Regular, Balanced or Specific.

- Listen to the feedback all the way through without judging it or jumping to a defensive response, both of which can mean that the feedback has been misunderstood.

- Try not to explain compulsively why you did something or even explain away positive feedback. Hear others' feedback as *their* experiences of you. Often it is enough to hear the feedback and say 'thank you'.

- Ask for feedback you are not given but would like to receive.

- It is helpful to get into the habit of asking your supervisees questions such as: 'What has been useful in this session?' and 'What has been less helpful in this session?'

If you can then receive and respond constructively to this feedback, the working relationship with your supervisees will be sustained even through bumpy periods, and everyone will benefit.

The challenges of giving and receiving feedback

A bottom line for supervisors is to consider the well-being of all who use the service where the supervisee works. When you give feedback ineffectively or your supervisees seem unable to receive it, there is a real danger of poor practice continuing and impacting on the patients or clients and the workplace.

When a supervisee seems unable to act on feedback and you have concern about their abilities as a practitioner, you may find it even harder to be direct and clear. This is particularly relevant when the relationship is not well established or you fear the extremes of your own judgements. In these situations you might find yourself pushing down your deeper concerns, and offering feedback that is vague, general or inconsistent. Even more serious is when a supervisor gives positive feedback despite having major concerns. While it is important to identify supervisees' strengths, encouragement is also about enabling personal growth through identifying areas for further development. When you can provide a climate of equality and encouragement, your supervisees are able to take risks and learn from mistakes in constructive ways and without fear.

Reflection point

What are your goals for the future when you *give* feedback? What are your goals for the future when you *receive* feedback?

Recommended reading

Millar, A. (2009) 'Developing skills: Practice, observation and feedback.' In P. Henderson (ed.) *Supervisor Training: Issues and Approaches.* London: Karnac Books.

This chapter (pp.107–22) identifies essential skills and attitudes needed for constructive and encouraging feedback in supervision.

CHAPTER 7

Supervising Trainees

> **Key points**
> - Supervision for trainees requires authoritative attention to both the training and placement contexts.
> - The supervisor's responsibilities as a gatekeeper to the profession create a risk of authoritarian interventions.
> - The supervisor must take account of the developmental level of trainees.

You will become a first image in the 'internal supervisor' of any trainee, part of their blueprint of what a supervisor should be like – or not like, when you get it wrong. So supervising trainees is a particularly responsible role. You may also be acting as a gatekeeper for your profession by passing or failing a trainee's practice. This is sometimes an uncomfortable balance of responsibility. Assessment and feedback underpin the working relationship with trainees.

> **Reflection point**
> Recall your first day of work in your profession, and how you felt. Now notice what your image of a 'trainee' is, and what kind of person you expect a trainee to be.

Usually trainees bring many transferable skills. If you explore these skills when contracting for the work, and value them, you will encourage the trainee who is likely to be worried about their capacity to do the work.

At the contracting stage, it is essential to establish key practicalities:

- What does the training agency or professional body expect of you?

- Is the frequency of meetings prescribed?

- What must you do to assess the trainee?

- Do you have to write a report or complete competence summaries?

- What do they want you to do if the trainee is not likely to pass the placement or work experience, or if you discover very unsafe work?

- Do you need to attend any meetings with the course trainer(s)?

- Who will allocate work to the trainee, and who will assess risk in terms of the trainee's readiness to work with any given presenting problem?

Some supervisors of trainees in placement are insufficiently in touch with the training course, and are therefore uncertain about course requirements. Making the responsibilities and requirements clear between all parties really helps both trainee and supervisor.

CASE STUDY: AN AUTHORITATIVE INTERVENTION

After prolonged difficulty, Joanne has found her own counselling placement, and says they will not allow her to bring any notes out of the building or let her make audio recordings of her work with clients. She seems vague about the details of the first case she brings to the supervision session. It is a course requirement that the supervisor hears about her work. She is desperate to pass the course and to make use of this placement opportunity. The supervisor's responsibility, though, is to clients, the course and the trainee. Resolution comes only through direct contact, with Joanne's permission, between the course and the placement, clarifying course requirements and inviting the placement to sign a written agreement that details mutual expectations.

Recording the supervision session (see Chapter 11) and then listening to it together or alone can demonstrate for supervisees of all levels of experience the value of recording. This can support the supervisee to notice what was unnoticed in the session, find new insights about the client or their self, accept what was unacceptable, and move to an observer position of both the work and the supervision (North 2013).

Practicalities about organisational placements

If you have any influence in the decision, consider the following:

- How many trainees can you place at one time and offer sufficient oversight of their work?

- What will they gain from your particular setting?

- What theoretical orientation (for counsellors or therapists) or approach fits with your work setting and your preferences as a supervisor?

- How can you avoid contributing to confusion for the trainee who serves many masters: you, the other staff in a placement, the training course and sometimes the demands of the professional body? If more than one person is supervising the work, consider why the other may be giving the trainee different comments.

- How far are you 'clinically responsible' in a placement for the work of the trainee?

You may not be legally responsible if the trainee is the subject of complaint, but you should know the steps to take in the placement or with the training organisation if you have serious concerns about a trainee's work. In this case, a written record of such concerns is essential.

Shame and power

Making mistakes and 'not knowing' are essential prerequisites for learning. The initial contract invites the trainee to bring any errors honestly to you. Research in the USA shows that material that could be central to learning and competency development is often not mentioned; this includes personal issues raised by clinical work, perceived clinical mistakes and negative reactions to clients (Ladany et al. 1996). So it is useful to say something like this to your supervisee:

> In supervision it is important to bring me things you are worried about, or feel you have not done quite right, or that you need to know more about. If you avoid bringing any of these worries, I shall be concerned that you are not telling me essentials. I will be clear with you as we go along if I have

any concerns about your ability to pass this course, and will discuss this with you long before I write any report.

> **Reflection point**
> Recall your early days in training. What sorts of issues did you avoid mentioning? How could the supervisor have made it easier for you to bring these issues to supervision?

As a supervisor you need to be able to name uncomfortable issues and offer assessments of the supervisee's practice. To do this, notice the interventions the trainee most commonly uses and the skills they have, as well as those they have yet to develop. This increases the trainee's commitment to work from strengths and also to repair gaps or become more self-aware, to encourage safer practice. In contrast, it is a shocking truth that some trainees reach the end of a placement believing their practice is satisfactory, only to be failed in the final course report. This should never happen. In addition, the trainee must know the steps to take if they wish to make a complaint about the supervisor. (This information can be clearly indicated in the initial contract.) It takes great courage to do so, and the power balance is such that oppressive behaviour often goes unchecked. This can be particularly insidious if either the trainee or the supervisor is from a minority and the other is not.

Developmental stage and training background

Compare your background experience and stage of development as a supervisor and practitioner with that of the supervisee. How good a 'fit' is it regarding any differences in your stage of development, training and theoretical approach? What kind of difficulties might you anticipate here? How will you signpost and deal with these difficulties if they occur? You can find out more about developmental models by reading the work of Stoltenberg and Delworth (1987), Inskipp and Proctor (1995) or Hawkins and Shohet (2012).

Developmental stages of the supervisee

You need to be flexible and adapt your supervisory interventions according to the differing developmental stage and needs of your supervisees. The needs that should be met are as follows:

* A new trainee needs structured containment of anxiety, support, encouragement and guidance, as well as explicit teaching.
* An experienced trainee needs less structured input but plenty of emotional support in the face of mistakes, and explicit feedback about work effectiveness and training requirements.
* A recently qualified practitioner needs both validation and challenge, along with a balance between teaching and encouragement of reflection and more collegial sharing.
* An experienced practitioner needs facilitation of self-exploration and self-challenge. Use more immediacy and creative approaches. Work with contextual complexities.

Skovholt and Ronnestad (1992) note that most development of cognitive *complexity* in counsellors occurs *after* formal training. These supervisees may swing emotionally between feeling very confident one moment and unsure the next, and still need feedback. The balance of support and challenge shifts too, as sometimes the newly qualified practitioner becomes anxious once more without the support of a course or placement behind them. Ronnestad and Skovholt (2012) describe development from rule-based approaches becoming less rigid as years pass. The process of learning that may begin with imitation and correction progresses to creative learning.

Reflection point
What are your specific concerns when you think about supervising a novice practitioner as compared with a supervisee at the later stages of their training?

Doing assessment collegially

Is your trainee meeting expected milestones on the placement? It is useful to take stock together at the beginning, explain what 'counts' as meeting the course criteria and offer regular, continuous transparent feedback based on your observations. Professional practice assessment can be done live, or through recorded materials with written commentary, and include reflection by the trainee (see Chapter 11).

Competences refer to observable performance; these can encourage the trainee to be their own first assessor by recording and critiquing their work to demonstrate that they have met the competence. Some trainees have to complete a written case study and this can form a good basis for detailed supervision of one particular working relationship. Other trainees keep learning journals so they record on a regular basis what went well and what did not. This builds good habits of self-monitoring. If you and the trainee share your observations and records, your report is easier to write and has no surprises for the trainee; however, there is a jump from developmental (known as formative) to final (summative) assessment. The trainee may be developing, but too slowly or unreliably to pass all the relevant practice elements of the training course.

Sensitive, fragile or defensive supervisees are those in greatest need of clear, firm, respectful and detailed feedback. The most common reasons for trainees in 'people work' to fail a training course arise from interpersonal or intrapersonal elements (Brear, Dorrian and Luscri 2008). The impact of such failure on self-esteem, or even on a sense of identity, can be profound. Clarity about what steps *must* be taken is essential. Moreover, if the person is unsuitable for the role, but lacks insight about this, a simple statement of the facts and your opinion may suffice, however uncomfortable it may be for both of you. Ensure you have documented your rationale: some such trainees might take out a complaint.

Being authoritative

Authoritative interventions include advice giving, providing information and confronting. Feedback can be particularly useful when the other person has a blind spot and is totally unaware of their motivation for what they have done or the impact of it. Often trainees fail to recognise minor ethical difficulties.

CASE STUDY: BEING AUTHORITATIVE

Rose cancelled a session with a vulnerable parent at short notice when her car broke down, without consideration for the parent's needs for continuity and reliability. The supervisor used her ethical framework to discuss the issue, and then said, 'In future I really want you to consider alternatives thoroughly before you cancel a session at such short notice. How will you make sure you do that?'

A supervisory style that is authoritative without being oppressive holds the service users and supervisee in mind. It is important to distinguish between mistakes, malpractice and poor practice. Minor mistakes are normal unintended slips in normally good practice. Malpractice arises when the practitioner meets their own needs at the expense of the workplace or people in it, and if it continues, this must be addressed. Poor practice may signal developmental needs or excessive pressures on the practitioner. It does require discussion. Being explicit about your intentions ('I want you to...') and summarising the conversation at intervals will help to keep a matter-of-fact tone. In this way you can lower the temperature of the exchange and keep the exploration on track.

Reflection point
How prepared do you feel to be confidently authoritative with trainees? What skills would you have to practise to increase your confidence?

Endings are important, too, and when the end of the course looms, the trainee may be facing a lot of loss, including their relationship with you. Talk about it, and what the balance of feelings may be about it. Despite the potential difficulties, remember that most supervision of trainees is delightful and mutually satisfying.

Recommended reading

Scaife, J. (2009) *Supervision in Clinical Practice* (2nd ed.)
Hove: Routledge

> See especially Chapter 14 on challenge and the
> assessment role. Although written for clinical
> psychologists, this chapter complements the advice we
> give in Chapter 6.

CHAPTER 8

Using Creative Methods

Key points

- Drawing on our creative right-brain functions can enhance the supervision process.
- Creative approaches can touch on the supervisee's personal issues, and careful contracting is important.
- There are many different sensory processes that can be adapted creatively for each supervisee's situation.

We experience the world through many senses: visual imagery, body responses, tactility, hearing and smell, as well as the more mysterious 'sixth' sense or intuition. Using these senses can often be of particular help when we feel stuck with an issue in supervision. Here creative processes can enable you and your supervisees to move towards more playful exploration where new landscapes and wisdom can be discovered. Everyone has their unique way of experiencing and learning from the world. Identifying your own and your supervisees' preferred modes, whether primarily visual, aural, verbal, physical or intellectual, will help you be in tune with your supervisees in this creative process.

Reflection point

Recall a moment as a child or adult when you felt engaged in a playful activity, however seemingly ordinary. What stands out for you in terms of the sensory mode you were using most, your mood at the time and the discoveries you made?

The brain's left hemisphere provides verbal reasoning, rationality and linear analytic functions. The right hemisphere processes emotion, intuition and non-verbal creativity, functions that are still given less credence in our apparently ultra-rational Western society. While we clearly need activity in both hemispheres for our learning and development, we can deepen the reflective process in supervision by also drawing on the treasure trove of our right-brain's emotional intelligence. Here are some creative processes that can be used and combined in a myriad of ways:

- metaphor/imagery/visualisation
- using small objects or cards to represent people, institutions, abstract issues or relationships
- drawing and painting
- creative writing and storytelling
- role play.

Reflection point

List some creative approaches you have experienced in any aspects of your work. What suited you best?

Contracting for using creative methods

Using creative methods can mean that you get to the heart of the matter very quickly. Sometimes this may have unpredictable and surprising outcomes, and touch on your supervisee's personal issues. Here it is important to note the difference between the use of creative methods in supervision and those used with clients. Your aim in the use of creative processes is to explore the supervisee's work with the client, keeping the focus on the supervisory frame. While you will be offering some direction, it is your supervisee who will be deciding how much personal 'stuff' to reveal. So as with all supervision procedures, careful collaborative negotiation and informed consent are essential. If you anticipate using creative methods, you need to discuss this beforehand. Then at each session you would contract afresh, using these methods only with your supervisee's full consent, having first explained what the exercise involves. Pacing the work carefully, giving sufficient time for debriefing and space for reflection afterwards is also essential.

Starting out using creative methods

Creative approaches, such as visualisation, role play and writing, can be used without any special props; however, you may wish to assemble a basic 'toolkit' of inexpensive materials that will be easily available to you and your supervisees during sessions. These could include small baskets of stones, buttons, shells, boxes of plastic or wooden bricks – or more clearly identifiable objects such as toy figures, animals and vehicles. Paper and coloured pens and pastels, differing textured material and a collection of picture postcards are invaluable standbys. Extending the toolkit further could include pliable materials, such as clay or playdough, or a small sandtray as a context for objects.

Creativity and 'The Three Paradoxes'

Gillie Bolton (2001) in her exploration of reflective practice captures the paradoxical nature of creativity when she writes that we need to:

- let go of certainty in order to acquire confidence
- look for something when we do not know what it is
- begin to act when we don't know how we should act.

So if you are new to using creative methods, it could feel quite daunting to join your supervisee in an exploration when neither of you are quite sure where it will lead. To build your confidence it is obviously helpful to have experience of these methods yourself. The exercise below offers some ways you can begin that can also be used as a form of self-supervision.

Exercise: Creative reflection

Reflect on an aspect of your own work using one of the following simple creative processes:

* *Using objects*: Gather together some small objects - buttons, shells, old keys, toy bricks. Reflect on a specific incident at work, perhaps a meeting, or a situation with a client. Represent this using the objects. Leave for about 15-30 minutes and then come back and see the arrangement afresh. Is there anything that stands out and offers you a new vista?

- *Imaging and metaphor*: Identify a client or supervisee. Sitting quietly with eyes closed, imagine if the person was an animal, what would they be? Without censorship, let the first image come to your mind. What is this animal doing? Now bring an image of yourself as an animal into this same setting. What kind of animal are you and how are you responding to the other one? What do you notice? Are there any new insights into what is going on between you? Are there any changes you would like to make?
- *Writing*: Reflect on a work situation where things feel stuck. Focus on one particular aspect and write down a newspaper headline that sums up the situation in a few words. Now give yourself journalistic licence to write a new headline that captures an ideal scenario, representing how you would like things to be. Notice what you would be doing differently in the new scenario.

Applying creative approaches in supervision

Chapter 5 outlined Hawkins and Shohet's (2012) 'seven-eyed model', which identifies different areas that are helpful to keep in mind when supervising. Drawing on their work, here are just a few suggestions for creative methods that could be introduced to your supervisees in the flow of the session:

1. *Focus on the client.* Invite your supervisee to close their eyes (only if this feels safe for them to do) and, focusing particularly on the first minutes of a recent session, *visualise the client.* Ask your supervisee to describe the client, identifying what they noticed most vividly (without analysis or assumptions). Use this as a base from which to gain new perceptions. You could also ask the supervisee to 'be the client', inviting them to take a *physical*

posture that captures their experience of the client. Then give space for the supervisee to reflect on this experience and identify any new learning. In these types of *embodied exercises* make sure you give time and space for your supervisee to 'de-role'.

2. *Focus on practice interventions.* Supervisees often need help to think 'outside the box' regarding interventions with their clients. A simple approach is to invite a free-flowing *brainstorming* of a few minutes that actively permits seemingly daft or outrageous, and possibly judgemental, suggestions. You can also join in, perhaps adding some crazy notions, to encourage a sense of being playfully alongside the supervisee. Your supervisee can then look at what has been written and use this as a springboard for decisions about new options that could possibly be rehearsed through role play.

3. *Focus on the relationship between the client and supervisee.* When the supervisee brings relationship challenges, it is important to help them stand outside the situation to get a new perspective. A helpful visualisation exercise is to ask your supervisee: 'Imagine you and your client were stranded together on a desert island. What positions are each of you taking on the island? How does this feel? What, if anything, would you like to be going differently and how will you get there?' Inskipp and Proctor (2001) suggest inviting the supervisee to *draw the client as a fish* (everyone seems able to draw a fish!). After the supervisee has shared their own reflections on the 'client' fish, they can add themselves to the same picture in the form of

another fish, or whatever image comes to mind, and then explore what stands out from the picture.

4. *Focus on the supervisee.* You can help your supervisees identify how their own issues and past relationships may be getting mixed up in the work with their clients by using the following four-stage process (Hawkins and Shohet 2012, p.96):

Stage 1   Ask your supervisee to *choose an object* to represent the client, and ask, 'Who does this person remind you of?'

Stage 2   Using an *empty chair* to represent the person they have identified, ask your supervisee what he or she would like to say to this person.

Stage 3   Invite your supervisee to describe all the ways in which their client is different from this person.

Stage 4   Ask your supervisee what they want to say now to their client – and if they wish to choose a different object to represent the client.

5. *Focus on the supervisory relationship.* As discussed in Chapter 9, there may be a 'parallel process' occurring in your relationship with the supervisee that actually reflects the supervisee's relationship with the client or a workplace issue. This could be a moment to ask, 'Could we stop for a moment and look at what's going on in the space between us right now?' If the supervisee is open to explore

further, you could both use *objects* or share *images* to represent your experience of what is happening.

6. *Focus on the supervisor.* Keeping all your *senses* open and being able to share them appropriately with your supervisee can often offer surprisingly helpful new perceptions. For example: 'I'm aware that I had a strong knotted feeling in my gut when you said that you felt fine when your client didn't turn up. I'm wondering if this reflects on any part of your relationship with the client, or maybe something going on here in supervision?'

7. *Focus on wider contexts.* Identifying the many contexts that impinge on the client work can be vividly brought to life through creative methods. A simple way is to invite the supervisee to choose objects to represent the many aspects and systems involved, thus creating a *three-dimensional map* that can be manipulated in the session.

> **Reflection point**
> Reflect on how you have started, or how you might wish to start, to use creative approaches in your supervisory work. Which methods feel most comfortable for you?

To summarise, here are some key pointers to keep in mind when using creative approaches:

- Make clear contracts for the work.

- Have materials at the ready so that they can be used with ease within the flow of the session.

- Keep an open and non-intrusive presence while the supervisee is working.

- Watch and listen carefully, drawing out the supervisee's experiences, rather than offering interpretation.

- Give space and time for your supervisees to offer their own reflections, and to 'de-role'.

Recommended reading

Lahad, M. (2000) *Creative Supervision*. London: Jessica Kingsley Publishers.

> This delightful book is full of creative, practical ideas for use in supervision across a range of disciplines.

Schuck, C. and Wood, J. (2011) *Inspiring Creative Supervision*. London: Jessica Kingsley Publishers.

> This jargon-free book offers clearly described techniques and processes that will inspire both the more experienced professional and those just starting out to use creative approaches in supervision.

CHAPTER 9

Working with Unconscious Processes

Key points

- Acknowledging the effects of unconscious communications in supervision is likely to increase its usefulness.
- Making intelligent, collaborative guesses about the 'unknown' is an effective practical strategy.
- Some basic psychological concepts can be used as tools to illuminate unconscious processes.

Unconscious thoughts and feelings are, by definition, unknown. In supervision, as in most forms of purposeful dialogue, 'talking things over' in a constructive way without any consideration of unconscious processes can usually develop greater understanding of the issue being discussed. But practical experience tells us that however cognitively sharp the supervisor is, and however clearly focused the contract with the supervisee, there are often 'other things going on' unconsciously, in and around the supervisory space, that can disrupt and distort the supervisor's and supervisee's best intentions.

> **Reflection point**
> Imagine you are providing fortnightly supervision for Stephen, a highly conscientious trainee, who prepares carefully for every session, always arrives punctually and makes notes of almost everything you say. Shortly before you are due to write a brief report for the tutor on his training course, Stephen starts to get in a muddle about dates, arrives late for sessions or forgets to bring his notebook. What do you think the problem might be?

The wisdom of not knowing

To help yourself and your supervisee become more conscious of what is happening – to look beneath the surface of events, to gain insight – you do not have to possess 'super-vision'. You can make informed guesses about what might be 'not yet in awareness' and keep these in mind as hunches. Exploring the unknown using intelligent guesswork is safe if it is tentative and correctable. In this collaborative, wondering mode as a supervisor you would be asking questions such as:

'What if…?'

'Could it be…?'

'How about the possibility that…?'

'Supposing you were feeling…?'

'I am feeling… and I wondered…'

'What else might explain…?'

Moving intentionally into this free-floating exploratory place might evoke intuitions or 'gut feelings' and perhaps a change in mood. This is when unconscious stuff may start 'bubbling up'. Intimations of embarrassment or mild anxiety – in you and/or your supervisee – can be a sign that some previously unsayable thought or unwanted feeling is coming into immediate awareness. It is sensible to accept and even welcome this kind of awkwardness, as it seems so often to indicate the emergence of important unconscious material. As a supervisor you need to know how to work *with* that discomfort. Ignoring it is an option, but you would risk missing some vital information about how your supervisee is dealing subjectively with the issue at hand.

The feeling that 'something else is going on' can become explicable with hindsight but is often hard to name and tricky to pin down. Unconscious dynamics – whether between two individuals only or within a group of people – are seldom neat and tidy. Wholeheartedly taking on the tasks of supervision, and fulfilling your ethical duty to act in the interests of the supervisee's clients, means being prepared at times to work with confusing and perhaps messy manifestations of unconscious processes. To help to bring these unconscious dynamics to awareness in supervision and make it easier to contain them, you need to be familiar with three very useful conceptual tools: the shadow, transference and parallel process.

The shadow

This powerful metaphor helps us to ponder 'the other side' of what goes on between people. It is based partly on the psychological idea that, acting on conclusions drawn unconsciously from experiences in early life, individuals put potential aspects of themselves – such as exuberance, melancholy, cleverness or anger – into their personal 'shadow bag' (Bly 1988, p.17), as if these particular qualities must be completely disowned and never witnessed by anyone. (It is important to note that the 'shadow bag' contains positive, as well as negative, human qualities.) What is really useful here is the idea of 'shadow projection'. For example, a supervisee who holds competitiveness in their personal shadow will probably be highly sensitive to competitive attitudes or behaviours in others, and strongly disapprove of, or severely judge, those people for being like that. The individual's own competitive self is unconsciously projected onto other people, where it is seen in a wholly negative light.

Another shadow concept to consider is when the disowned quality is not projected but remains hidden. A simple example of this could be: an efficient supervisor with a lot of respect for a highly skilled and ambitious supervisee is secretly very envious of their career path, and somehow never gets round to providing them with a reference for an exciting new job. We might guess that envy was buried deep in the supervisor's shadow as a totally unallowable emotion. Because it stayed unconscious, the supervisor was unable to acknowledge its effect, which was detrimental to the supervisee.

Reflection point

Looking again at the first reflection point above, what are your guesses about what could be emerging from the supervisee's shadow which might help to explain his surprising change in behaviour? (The impending report seems significant. Stephen sets extremely high standards for himself, so it may be useful to think about the shadow side of perfectionism.)

Transference

When a supervisee perceives their supervisor as an authority figure, like a parent or teacher, they will probably, unconsciously, be evoking a previous experience of such a relationship and 'transferring' it from the past into the present one. The relational phenomenon of transference is like a subliminal projection of assumptions and expectations onto the actual, immediate, conscious relationship. This process is not necessarily a barrier to doing good work, but it can be constricting. For instance, a supervisee who in childhood or adolescence had a teacher they constantly idealised might unconsciously expect or demand the same 'perfection' from their supervisor. In this case, the supervisor would be wise to notice the strong positive transference and then step off the pedestal where the supervisee is putting them. You might be tempted as a supervisor to bask in the 'halo effect' – being seen as all-knowing, faultless, even saintly – but this would be doing your supervisee no favours. If they hang onto your every word, they are unlikely to discover their own wisdom or develop authentic expertise.

In practice, the effect of transference is usually experienced as a persistent pattern of misunderstanding or misperception. An example would be when a supervisee hears every supervisory query as an implied criticism. They automatically translate a question such as 'What were you thinking about when you chose that intervention?' into 'You chose the wrong intervention.' This supervisee's negative transference onto the supervisor is perhaps one of a critical parent, so instead of perceiving the supervisor as genuinely interested in their work, they feel interrogated and judged.

The best practical response to transference is simply to point it out and wonder aloud about it. In the example above, the supervisor might say:

> There is an aspect of our communication I would like to explore with you. Tell me if I'm wrong, but I get the impression you often hear my questions as negatively critical. If so, I want you to know that is not my intention at all. Perhaps it's my tone of voice? Or something else? I am really interested in understanding this better. How would you like to approach this so we can find out more?

Something important to watch out for when addressing the supervisee's transference is your own internal reaction to the projection. For instance, the halo effect referred to above could produce unexpected feelings of irritation and exasperation towards the supervisee, or it might seduce you into believing you really are a perfectly wonderful supervisor. Being ascribed god-like powers is very likely to generate a strong counter-transference in you, one way or another!

Reflection point

Recall a time when you had a supervisor with whom you felt inexplicably uncomfortable. What relational pattern from your past might you have been unconsciously transferring into the relationship? Similarly, if you had a supervisor you placed high on a pedestal, what transference might have been taking place?

As a supervisor you need to bring all your self-awareness into play in order to detect the signs of transference. A starting point is to notice when and how you get 'pulled out of shape' in a session with a supervisee. For instance, you find yourself talking unusually fast and becoming over-helpful, or feeling strangely squashed and flattened, or perhaps just very sad or anxious for no obvious reason. Such an effect may come from the supervisee directly in their relationship with you, or it may originate outside the supervisory space in the supervisee's work. This is when it is very helpful to know how unconscious processes can operate in parallel.

Parallel process

For many decades, particularly in mental health and social care professions, supervisors have noticed a curious phenomenon in their work with supervisees. In the simplest terms, this occurs when, without conscious intention, the supervisor–supervisee relationship replicates or reveals something happening unconsciously in the supervisee–service user relationship. The phrase 'something happening' is deliberately vague. As a manifestation of unconscious communication, usually with strong emotional content, parallel process does not lend itself readily to precise formulations; yet its practical application as an interpretative tool is so valuable in supervision that it is well worth developing the knack of noticing parallel process effects and commenting on them. Sometimes parallel process is obvious and unmistakable, but more often it is subtle and ambiguous, so you will definitely need your 'radar' switched on to detect it (see 'Eye 6' in Chapter 5).

CASE STUDY: PARALLEL PROCESS IN ACTION

Carlos is a counsellor at a sixth form college. In a session with his supervisor, Owen, he brings the case of a young woman he is counselling following the suicide of one of her close male friends. As Carlos talks about his client and her bereavement, Owen hears Carlos's voice becoming flat and monotonous. He also notices how stiffly Carlos is sitting in his chair and making no eye contact, which is unlike him. At the same time, Owen is aware of growing unusually irritated and even angry for no apparent reason. Feeling 'pulled out of shape' now, Owen continues to listen while considering saying something about this to Carlos. When Carlos mentions that he finds the client incredibly calm and poised, Owen forms a hunch about what his increasing irritation might mean, and decides to interrupt.

Their ensuing discussion identifies a parallel process. Hearing Owen reveal his sense of rising anger leads Carlos to acknowledge his unstated frustration with the client, who he says also sat very still and spoke in a monotone. When presenting the client, Carlos had unconsciously replicated the client's apparent disconnection from her strong feelings about her loss. Referring to the angry sensation he began to experience when listening to Carlos describe her, Owen wonders if he was paralleling how she felt towards her friend for ending his life. It is possible that her unexpressed emotion regarding his suicide - her anger perhaps masked by her unwaveringly calm poise - had been unconsciously received by Carlos, who unknowingly transmitted it to Owen. After talking about this, Carlos and Owen no longer feel frustrated or angry. Their compassion for the client is restored, and Carlos has gained some insight into where the client might be getting stuck in her grieving process.

It is important to understand that if a supervisee is very anxious or angry about a situation (such as the unethical behaviour of a colleague) and the supervisor, on hearing the story, feels likewise, this is *not* a parallel process – it is simply two people having the same reaction to something! The concept of parallel process is also wrongly used to describe events in which the parties involved have had similar experiences (e.g. the recent birth of a grandchild); they may well end up 'mirroring' each other in some way, but that is *not* parallel process.

While many supervisors take the view that transference and parallel process effects are a regular and necessary part of supervisory work, others are not always so convinced of their usefulness. All supervisors would agree, however, that 'strange happenings' in the supervisory relationship deserve close attention. Without some form of acknowledgment and exploration, an odd event or peculiar feeling can become 'an elephant in the room' – filling the space and getting in the way of clear vision. In practice, we find that applying psychological concepts like transference and parallel process respectfully and tentatively within supervision can not only 'clear the air' and shed light on specific situations, but also deepen our general understanding of the unconscious dimension in everyday working relationships.

Recommended reading

Egan, G. (2013) *The Skilled Helper* (10th ed.). Pacific Grove, CA: Brooks/Cole.

> Nearly every chapter in this hugely influential book, which focuses on problem management, contains a section on the shadow side of helping.

Kahn, M. (2001) *Between Therapist and Client*. New York, NY: Owl Books.

This is a highly readable account of how transference works 'intersubjectively' and what to do with it in actual practice.

CHAPTER 10

Putting Ethics into Practice

> **Key points**
> - Ethical principles work as guides in particular contexts, helping you to move beyond reaction to reflection.
> - The supervisor creates an 'ethical field' to enable collaborative enquiry with supervisees.
> - Dialogues about dilemmas can provide opportunities for growth and learning.
> - Ethically minded supervision includes authoritative challenge as well as safe support for the supervisee.

Supervisory ethics are all about the 'moral landscape' in which the work is done. A good supervisor needs to be an alert gardener in this sense – keeping an eye on small, emerging details while simultaneously surveying the whole scene to see how everything connects. Practising this watchful attention to 'specifics in context' helps to make abstract ethical principles, such as trustworthiness and autonomy, come alive as fruitful ideas, not just high-minded ideals.

For the ethical practitioner, context is everything. Formal codes of practice from across the helping professions (e.g. early years teaching, social work, clinical psychology and counselling) provide useful 'positioning' frameworks. In supervision we consider personal values, organisational policies and local protocols as distinctive features in a moral map of the field in which the supervisee is working, and we can use them to help us find 'the right way to go'. This collaborative movement explores possible paths from different perspectives. Without the guidance created by this kind of 'multi-visioning' – which includes supervision of supervision (see Chapter 14) – we might get seriously lost.

What makes supervision so compelling is that there can often seem to be very few straight lines and many hidden or 'grey areas' in the supervisory landscape. Uncertainty, confusion and strongly ambivalent feelings can arise in this space. It is surely significant that in the literature of supervision, several emotive terms regularly cluster around the word 'ethics' (e.g. dilemma, harm, breach of confidentiality, gross misconduct, duty of care, grievance and malpractice). As an example, a conscientious and highly competent counselling psychologist who was complained against by a client came to supervision feeling a mixture of anxiety, guilt and shame about the case for months.

Dealing with such challenging issues in supervision often raises the emotional temperature. Timely engagement of ethical thinking helps to contain these forceful feelings so that we can find a reasoned *response* to the situation in hand and not get stuck in a *reaction* to it. Although practical outcomes from reactivity may not be inherently unethical, *reflexivity* is a much more reliable basis for sound ethical practice.

Exercise: Giving space for reaction, reflection and action

In each of the following scenarios, imagine you are the practitioner's supervisor. Notice your likely reaction (feelings), reflection (thoughts) and considered response (actions).

* There has been a spate of burglaries on the estate served by the GP surgery where Gaynor is a counsellor. A patient in counselling tells Gaynor he knows who the thief is and where the stolen property has been stashed.

* After running a busy corporate coaching practice for five years, Marsha reports feeling run down and tired all the time. She is separating from her husband. Her mother died a year ago and Marsha has responsibility for the care of her father. She says she cannot afford to stop working, not even for a week.

* Imran, a mental health adviser in a student support service, has been told by one of the female students he is helping that she has strong feelings for him. She has been suicidal in the recent past. He has said he finds her attractive and is very concerned for her welfare if he rejects her.

In supervision the ethical stance is often one of slowing down or stopping, in order to see better, to step back and reflect – and, if no-one is in danger, simply perhaps to wait. Hard-working supervisees whose habitual preferences propel them into immediate problem solving and quick decision making may get irked at this point, but a sustained pause for reflection is nearly always useful in building ethical capacity. On the other hand, deeply committed practitioners who tend to linger long in 'thoughtful indecision' may need to be prompted into decisive action through the supervisor's authoritative input.

Cultivating an ethical field

How do we define the grounds for ethical reflection in practical terms? Common sense is surely indispensable, but the supervisory role is founded on much more than that. You might find it useful to think of a field created by, and containing, the following four connected elements: contracting, legality, policies and stakeholders.

Contracting

Your contracts with supervisees form the bedrock of ethical dialogue. As described in Chapter 2, the safe support of the supervisory relationship is greatly enhanced when expectations and assumptions (the 'implicit' contract) are voiced and clarified as much as possible. This sense of safety is especially valuable when you need to challenge the supervisee on an ethically questionable aspect of their practice. A mutually negotiated contract makes a difficult conversation easier. For example, at the initial contracting stage, you might ask your supervisee, 'What would you want me to do if I had any concerns about your work?' – a respectful and empowering question that can sow the seeds of a genuinely co-operative relationship.

Legality

Ethically sound practice is, of course, informed by statutory obligations and legal requirements. Reasonable decisions made in the reflective space of supervision can be constrained by the laws of the land, since what might be considered highly ethical within one domain is not necessarily legal in another, and vice versa (Jenkins 2007).

It goes without saying that supervision of individuals or teams working with children must be rooted in child protection and safeguarding law. In the UK it is rare for supervisors in the helping professions to be directly involved in court cases, but it is essential as a supervisor to know where you stand concerning access to notes and records of supervision. We do not have to be lawyers to be good supervisors, but we do need to know where to find up-to-date information on pertinent legal cases and, if necessary, to seek expert advice. (See the Recommended reading list at the end of this chapter.)

Policies

Just as state legislation firmly plants some 'hard facts' in our ethical field, a professional code of practice and an organisation's policy handbook can be regarded as 'soft law'. These are the rules about what actions are prohibited or required according to ethical principles. Get to know the context-specific codes and guidelines your supervisees are expected to follow in their working roles; these institutional documents may not be page-turners, but they are invaluable as dry fertiliser for the ethical ground you are tending.

Reflection point
What would you do if an organisation your supervisee is employed by did not have a written policy regarding confidentiality? To your mind, would this mean the organisation was inherently unsafe? If so, as an external supervisor what might you do about it?

Stakeholders

Last but definitely not least: people! In a supervision session focused on a point of ethics it is always helpful to identify everyone who holds a stake in the outcome. It is rarely the supervisee's client or patient only. The values, perspectives, agendas and goals of many other parties may all come into play if there is a major ethical issue to be addressed. When there are conflicts of interest, the supervisor and supervisee might have to dig deep to find the common ground. Your supervisory ability to take an overview as well, as if 'helicoptering' above the ethical field, is also critical. In practice, the insight that brings about the 'felt sense' of what is ethically sound can come from any direction, so it makes sense to populate the scene you are surveying with all the relevant voices.

Developing 'dilemmability'

Ethically minded supervision tends not to take a binary view of things. What is often called 'black-and-white thinking' may be productive at times, but it inevitably pre-empts our critical grey areas of thought, from where new or renewed ideas emerge. This growthful source is a vital factor in developing ethical maturity (Carroll and Shaw 2012) and is activated each time a dilemma is brought into the field. The following are three examples of causes brought to supervision:

1. Siobhan is counselling Roy, a recently bereaved train driver, who says he has been experiencing panic attacks at work. He insists that she not inform his employer (who is paying for his counselling,

following his wife's death) as he might be taken off the job he loves.

2. A supervisee working in a hospice reports being bullied and sexually harassed by a senior manager, whom she names, trusting in your confidentiality. The supervisee does not know that this manager is a colleague with whom you are close.

3. Pawel, a trainee youth worker, tells you he caught 11-year-old Conor taking money from the till in the community centre's café. Pawel says he let him keep it because he knows that Conor's mother, a registered heroin user, is vulnerably housed and struggling to stay in their home.

Literally meaning a 'double assumption', a dilemma simultaneously provokes and thwarts a 'right/wrong' answer. Practically speaking, ethics do not always give us direct answers, but they do provide us with signposts towards *possible* answers. As a supervisor you gain familiarity with the relevant signs and come to recognise the paths, even though you might not know exactly where they lead. Your role invites you to be calmly hopeful at each step.

Reflection point

Even if you were absolutely sure of the best course of action to recommend in scenarios like the three briefly described above, how useful for the supervisee would it be just to tell them directly? What might be the advantages and disadvantages of 'making their decision for them'? What kind of supervisory process would ensure they learn something new from the situation?

A great tool for assisting a supervisee to refresh or develop their 'dilemmability' is Socratic questioning (see also Chapter 6) – essentially posing open, reflective, leading questions like those in the previous Reflection point box. For example, Siobhan could be asked:

> 'How will it affect your contract with the organisation if you do not disclose this information about Roy?'

> 'What do you think are the risks involved in not telling the employer about the panic attacks?'

> 'How does maintaining Roy's confidentiality about this issue support him to resolve his grief?'

> 'What is your fantasy of what someone else would do to resolve the dilemma?'

> 'What other options are there?'

These supervisory questions use the dilemma as a growth point to help the supervisee extend their ethical capacity.

Addressing fitness to practise

Part of the supervisor's role is to act as a gatekeeper for the profession. Trainee practitioners are especially aware of this when coming for supervision, as the report you write about their work could directly affect their entry into their chosen professional field. Whether a supervisee is in training or fully qualified, if you have concerns about their competence and resilience, you clearly have an ethical responsibility to address the concerns, in the interests of protecting clients or patients from possible harm. Your ethical position as supervisor is also one of support and care for the supervisee. There are two key questions here: (a) Should this supervisee be carrying this workload at this time? and (b) Should this supervisee be working at all?

When a competent supervisee tells you about their health problems, a recent bereavement or a family crisis, for example – and possibly all three at once – you can propose a practical risk assessment. This would focus equally on the welfare of the service users and the supervisee's self-care. It might lead to the supervisee taking time off, or working fewer hours, or getting some personal therapy or other reliable, boundaried support – whatever will help them to serve their clients' or patients' best interests and be least likely to do harm.

If a supervisee seems unaware of, or is unwilling to discuss, their apparent difficulties with performing the required tasks of supervision, this might be a good time to consult confidentially with a trusted colleague before confronting the supervisee. Consider a second opinion before acting decisively. It is hard to tell someone they must seriously improve their game; even harder to ask them to stop playing altogether. This standard-setting confrontation process is intended to:

- invite or persuade the supervisee to reflect on and assess the state of their current practice

- give them your assessment with reference to their professional code of conduct or organisational policy

- set out their immediate options

- support them to make the best ethical decision; you would then amend or end your contract accordingly.

This chapter began with an analogy between supervision and gardening, and now is a good time to remember that a well-tended garden is usually a very pleasant place in which to sit and listen and reflect – even though (as every keen gardener knows) there are always a variety of jobs to do at any one time. The 'ethical field' in supervision is likewise an ever-changing space, with prickly things coming and going along with delightful bursts of new growth. Maintaining this fertile space is one of the great satisfactions of working as a supervisor.

Recommended reading

Bond, T. and Mitchels, B. (2008) *Confidentiality and Record Keeping in Counselling and Psychotherapy*. London: Sage and BACP.

> This is an invaluable resource for considering every aspect of confidential records and achieving best practice.

Hawkins, P. and Shohet, R. (2012) *Supervision in the Helping Professions* (4th ed.). Maidenhead: Open University Press (McGraw-Hill).

> Chapter 9, entitled 'Ethics and Facing Challenging and Complex Situations in Supervision', is a helpful reflection on ways of responding to ethical challenges.

Mitchels, B. and Bond, T. (2008) *Legal Issues Across Counselling and Psychotherapy Settings*. London: Sage and BACP.

> This book contains detailed information on a range of legal matters relevant to 'people practitioners' working in all sectors, private and public, from voluntary agencies to statutory services.

Scaife, J. (2009) *Supervision in Clinical Practice (2nd ed.)*. Hove: Routledge.

> Chapter 7 is a very useful, well-referenced discussion of ethical dilemmas and issues in supervision.

CHAPTER 11

Using Communications Technology

Key points

- Recording offers immediate evidence of practice to help supervisees reflect accurately on their work.
- Supervising at a distance requires very practical attention to contracting.
- Using online technology highlights the importance of privacy and confidentiality in supervision.

This chapter describes the practical use of recordings in supervision, and using media such as email and Skype for conducting supervision. As noted in Chapter 7, audio and video recordings of trainees in the helping professions are used on many courses as tools for appraisal, reflection and learning. A supervisor of trainee counsellors, for example, is familiar with the process of listening to recordings of trainees' sessions with clients. Prior to any form of recording being made by a professional helper, every service user should be made fully aware of the purpose of the recording and who will be listening to it, and then invited to give their written consent. Client confidentiality must be carefully protected at every stage.

The confidentiality of media, whether recorded or not, is always of primary importance in supervision. Electronic or online communication can 'feel' private and discreet yet may not be secure from accidental or intentional intrusion. In addition to being ethically astute, any supervisor working via the Internet needs to be technologically fit and cybersmart to practise safely in this respect (Anthony and Nagel 2009).

> *Reflection point*
> What are your first thoughts about using some form of technology (telephone, recording device, email, etc.) as an integral part of your supervisory practice? How might you respond to a supervisee who asks you to be their online supervisor?

Recording for reflecting

Consider two different recordings: (a) a supervisee at work (e.g. holding a counselling session), and (b) a recording of a supervision session. How can these recordings be used most effectively by the supervisor to benefit the client and the practitioner? Some suggestions are given in the sections below.

A recording of a supervisee at work

First of all, the supervisor and the supervisee (e.g. a counsellor in training) agree on a well-defined plan for how the recording is to be used. Key points in their contract could include the following:

- The intention is for the counsellor to develop their skills in reflective practice by carrying out an honest self-assessment based on this specific session.

- The client is at the centre of the exercise, but the focus is mostly on the counsellor and how they respond to the client.

- The supervisor is not looking for 'perfection' or 'brilliance' but wants to see evidence of the counsellor's capacity for accurate reflection and constructive self-challenge.

- The counsellor listens to the recording and makes written notes before giving them, with the recording, to the supervisor.

- The counsellor's notes should convey what they consider they did effectively in the session, what they would like to do differently and where they feel a particular need for guidance.

- The supervisor listens to the recording, makes notes and then reads the counsellor's notes in preparation for the next supervision session.

- At the session the supervisor will offer feedback on (a) the counsellor's reflective notes, and (b) the counsellor's work as evidenced in the recording (i.e. the supervisor gives separate attention to an appraisal of the counsellor's self-assessment of their work).

- The supervisor and the counsellor agree on the counsellor's 'learning edge', what actions the counsellor could take to develop this and what form of supervisory follow-up would be most helpful.

In the case of audio-only recordings, it is of course necessary to appreciate that significant information is missing: seating arrangements, lighting, body language and other tangible factors are naturally inaudible. However, this apparent lack can be surprisingly beneficial in two ways. First, the practitioner becomes more aware of how they use their voice as they respond to the client, and the supervisor may offer some sensitive feedback on this. Second, the re-hearing of the client's actual words, and the enhanced attention paid to their language and imagery, often leads to increased understanding and insight. A further advantage for the client is that their own voice gets heard – literally – by their counsellor's supervisor, which (outside of the specialist field of family therapy, where a supervisor often observes sessions as they take place) normally never happens.

Reflection point
Imagine the thoughts and feelings a supervisee might have about a recording of their work being viewed or heard by their supervisor. (You may have been in this situation yourself as a trainee.) What can the supervisor do or say that will help the supervisee feel less anxious or embarrassed and more confident about the transparency of this process?

A recording of a supervision session
Continuing with the example of a trainee counsellor, how might a recording of a supervision session help to develop their skills and extend their learning? Assuming the supervisor is also ready to discover something new and

improve their own practice, a discussion of the recording could be of great practical benefit to both parties.

The supervisee:

- has an opportunity to review how they use their time in the session

- has a reliable record of specific feedback or factual information given by the supervisor

- can identify instances of helpful and unhelpful responses from the supervisor

- can decide in their own time on what they want to feed back to the supervisor and how to do it.

The supervisor:

- has an opportunity to review how they manage the supervisee's timekeeping

- has a record of how they delivered some feedback and how its content was received

- can identify instances of things being missed or muddled in the dialogue.

Setting aside precious supervisory time to discuss a recording of a supervision session might seem like a luxury. As a method of holding a meta-conversation ('talking about how we talk about things'), it certainly needs to be structured by the supervisor in a time-efficient way. In practice, this may be carried out using a recording just two or three times quite early in the work with the supervisee. After that, it is a good habit for the supervisor to raise the dialogue to the meta-conversational level for a part of each meeting (some supervisees will do this themselves anyway without any prompting). This ensures the vital two-way feedback channel is kept clear and open.

Interpersonal process recall

Based on collaborative work by Norman Kagan (1980), interpersonal process recall (IPR) is a well-researched technique for reassessing a dialogue or encounter, usually between two people, by means of a recording. For example, a counsellor brings to supervision a recording of a session with a client. In IPR terms the counsellor becomes the 'recaller' and the supervisor is the 'enquirer'. The recaller takes the lead in the process as they decide when to start and stop playing the recording throughout the supervision session. The enquirer asks open questions (e.g. 'What were you thinking or feeling just then?' 'What pictures or memories went through your mind at that point?' 'Is there anything you would have wished to do differently at that point?') designed to help the recaller go back to - and stay in - the 'there and then' of the counselling session. IPR regards the recaller as 'knowing more than they know' about their interpersonal processes, and the enquirer's job is to help them realise this, without interpretation or suggestion.

Supervising by telephone

The convenience of formally contracted regular telephone supervision is indisputable for practitioners who would otherwise have to travel long distances to see an appropriate supervisor, or whose mobility is limited due to disability or illness. As it avoids the need for transport, it is likely to be less expensive than most face-to-face meetings.

Practitioners living in large rural areas or sparsely populated regions can engage in 'distance supervision' by phone (or email; see below) with a supervisor in another part of the country. This helps to avoid the kind of dual relationships, both personal and professional, which inevitably arise in small communities and can compromise the boundaries of confidentiality.

Here are some other issues to consider:

- *Would you supervise someone you had never met in person?* A contract to provide telephone supervision might or might not begin with an initial face-to-face meeting. Unless geography rules it out completely, the relationship is likely to be strengthened by meeting together in person at the start, and also at planned intervals later as the supervisory work develops.

- *Would you consider supervising more than one person by phone simultaneously?* Voice-to-voice meetings with three or more people in different physical locations can be held easily via a free teleconferencing service. Group supervision (see Chapter 13) in this mode would require careful planning and pre-contracting. A group that meets regularly for face-to-face sessions might need a telephone alternative at times, for example, if severe weather conditions prevented a physical meeting.

- *Would you be available to your supervisees by phone at any time?* A contract for face-to-face supervision can include the provision of voice-to-voice contact in emergencies or when an immediate consultation is required. You would need to be clear with your supervisees about your 'normal office hours' and also (if you are practising independently) whether you would charge a professional fee for telephone calls between scheduled sessions.

Supervising by email

Your contract with supervisees must address the particular constraints of communicating by email. Unlike the telephone, e-supervision is asynchronous and involves you spending time on your own composing the messages (hopefully without interruptions, as in a face-to-face session). If you are a fluent writer and already accustomed to receiving lengthy or complex emails and reading them onscreen, you have two significant practical advantages in offering this service. It goes without saying that all emails should use encryption software to protect confidentiality. Practically speaking, it is advisable to keep a timetable and log the hours when you undertake e-supervision sessions within your working week. Consider the following points:

- *Writing style.* How important is the compatibility between your written style and your supervisees' styles? These styles may differ widely. Some individuals have a 'rough and ready' mode of expression in emails; others write with rigorously correct grammar and full punctuation. How might these expressive differences in the 'written voice' help or hinder an effective supervisory alliance? (See Chapter 3 for ideas about adapting your style in supervisory relationships.)

- *Time delay.* The inevitable gap between receiving an email from a supervisee and replying to it has a positive side effect: it creates a useful space for you to reflect or consult on the issues at hand and also to review the precise wording of your whole reply before actually sending it. Your contract with supervisees should include an agreement about the optimal length of intervals between emails from either direction, and a plan for what happens if connectivity is lost.

- *Organisation of notes and resources.* Using emails for supervision automatically provides a dated record of the supervisory work done, making it a simple task to retrieve all the mail that is pertinent to a particular supervisee. Here your email programme presents a distinct benefit when you review your supervisory work, as it will include all the attachments and links you sent to each supervisee. If you are also holding scheduled face-to-face meetings with supervisees, your notes of these sessions will need to be integrated with your email records.

Reflection point
If you decided to provide supervision by email, on what particular skills and experiences would you be drawing to help you work in this medium?

Live video supervision

Services such as Skype, VSee and other proprietary systems provide affordable ways to conduct synchronous sound-and-vision communication. Although group supervision via the Web is a relatively new development, one-to-one live video supervision sessions are familiar to many practitioners. People who are accustomed to 'Skyping' with friends or family living abroad, for example, do not find it difficult to adapt to the different online etiquette of a professional meeting. In practice, it is not unusual to encounter brief technical problems (mainly due to unreliable broadband connections), but the advantages of real-time distance supervision sessions remain persuasive for many clinical supervisors (Armstrong and Schnieders 2003).

Two practical issues to bear in mind are:

- *Technical competence.* Ensuring the secure and smooth running of Web-based communications requires a good level of up-to-date technical knowledge. It makes sense to network with other supervisors already working in this medium and share information about the pros and cons of different software and online services. Supervisees also need the know-how, and some may be more technically sophisticated than you, so be prepared to both teach and learn from those you are supervising.

- *Privacy of the physical space.* Whether you conceive of video supervision as a virtual meeting in cyberspace or regard it simply as an Internet-facilitated dialogue, both you and your supervisees still have to conduct it from a private physical location. The boundary around the online supervisory encounter may not always be clear or controllable. You might supervise someone sitting at their computer desk in an office shared with colleagues, who may come and go during a session; or the supervisee could be using a laptop in their home with the distracting sounds of family life in the background.

A final thought is that supervision is always supervision, regardless of whatever technology is employed to facilitate it. It would surely be a mistake to let the workings of supervisory relationships become defined by the communication technologies we use. The essential tasks and functions of supervision can be fulfilled with equal rigour in every medium.

Recommended reading

Driscoll, J. (2007) *Practising Clinical Supervision: A Reflective Approach for Healthcare Professionals* (2nd ed.). Oxford: Baillière Tindall.

> This book contains a usefully detailed chapter entitled 'Alternative Methods in Clinical Supervision: Beyond the Face-to-Face Encounter' drawing on practical experience of distance supervision in the USA and Australia as well as the UK.

Scaife, J. (2009) *Supervision in Clinical Practice (2nd ed.)*. Hove: Routledge.

> Chapter 10 provides a thoughtful discussion of the use of recordings and other technologies in supervision.

CHAPTER 12

Supervising People in Different Contexts and Roles

Key points
- Supervision can support teamwork and organisational thinking.
- In multi-disciplinary teams there may be many differences to consider.
- The culture of the organisation may value 'knowing' above 'reflecting'.

Supervision in organisations is often of time-limited work; therefore, risk assessment is essential and you need to discuss with your supervisees whether this is the right place, the right person and if there is enough time to do what is needed. In services where the organisation provides a free or reduced-rate service, there is usually a much wider span of social, cultural and economic difference than in self-employed work, so all staff should also be sensitive to issues of difference and consider the appropriateness of the theoretical model or helping intervention being offered.

You might work as a supervisor internal to the organisation as a member of a multi-disciplinary team (as clinical psychologists, nursery nurse managers and hospice workers often do). Here, or when supervising someone or a group from another professional background, your initial supervisory work can usefully examine assumptions, language and meaning, culture, norms and values (see Burnham's 'Social Graces' noted in Chapter 2). Language, for instance, is best kept simple. For example, saying 'I am not sure what this term means for you. For me it means... Tell me your version' is more productive than taking for granted that your definition is the only one. Never be afraid to ask for an explanation about a term being used. Pretending to understand something to avoid seeming ignorant or stupid is disrespectful to the supervisee and distracting for you. Sometimes you can take a role as interpreter and mediator between different professional groups who are working together, and this can be very valuable to the organisation.

Supporting teamwork

Team members are very reliant on each other but have different habits about, for instance, making notes immediately or consulting colleagues before taking actions that affect their relationship with the service user. Sometimes there is mutual respect in a team, but mutual misunderstanding, or even contempt, is equally possible. Yet a team has to agree about essentials of the work: *what* needs to be done in a difficult situation and *how* to do it. So a supervisor must develop a good grasp of team roles and responsibilities, and any significant individual's strengths and weaknesses as well. For example, a group of Macmillan nurses have to prioritise who is to get frequent visits, and for what. But they may be working alongside a doctor, an occupational therapist and a physiotherapist who all have their own roles and responsibilities for the patient. There may be a case meeting, but not all professionals are available to attend it. Some may dispute who needs immediate care and from whom, with some members seeing the patient as the person in focus and others focusing on the spouse or small child affected by the impending death.

When one member of the team does not write their notes, or does not share them with all team members, the others may not know the current situation, especially if the worker is away or ill. The supervisor of such a multi-disciplinary team may have to cool a heated discussion about what to do next without taking sides or ignoring poor practice. One creative way to lower the temperature would be to put a number of items on a table to represent individual members of the family and the multi-disciplinary team, and move them about to convey each person's take on the situation. This creative overview can shift the discussion from recrimination to problem solving.

Anxiety in the organisation

A supervisor can, and often does, play a major role in containing the anxieties of the workers they supervise, and their job is to sustain a safe yet rigorous reflective space. An 'anthropological' curiosity and a willingness not to judge can make big demands on you and your capacity for optimism. Realism is important, too: good supervision cannot compensate for inadequate facilities, poor management or unmotivated staff. In some places, a culture of blame may arise to allow distress to be projected onto others in or outside it (Stewart 2002). You need self-knowledge and a good understanding of your own attitudes regarding power and oppression. You need to consider the organisational culture and whether the espoused values are lived in actual practice.

Supervision is a space to explore 'not knowing', 'feeling stuck' and how to learn from mistakes. Yet most organisations expect staff and a supervisor to be knowledgeable and competent. In order to meet the challenge of working with your own and others' uncertainty, both supervisor and supervisee have to find 'The Courage to be Imperfect' (Dreikurs 1970). This requires reflecting on, rather than reacting to, the needs of clients or staff, or the demands of every new initiative that comes along. Saying 'I don't know' can be hard if you feel you *ought* to know. It is beneficial to tolerate the discomforts of not knowing while still thinking together about an issue: this models the reflective process and demonstrates the value of reflection to the supervisee.

In many service organisations, the worker or practitioner may have no choice of supervisor. The supervisor and supervisee may have to learn to engage with a relationship style in the other person that is not their most comfortable (see Chapter 3). Every supervisor needs to consider the impact of the organisation on the work, and how to establish a confidential conduit of feedback to the organisation within the agreed confidentiality base if serious bad practice is revealed.

Clinical governance

Supervisors may be senior members of staff in the organisation. Sometimes they both manage and provide case supervision to the same staff, which has its own demands on both parties. Many organisations therefore outsource reflection (Wonnacott 2011) and employ external supervisors. All supervisors have to take clinical governance into account: issues include ensuring safety of clients and staff; considering staff development needs; learning from mistakes; use of audit and outcome measures; and always holding in mind the views of service users.

> **Reflection point**
> What are the most obvious issues to address in your organisation when you are supervising workers there? What might you risk overlooking if you simply deal with the present individual and whatever direct work they are doing? How does the learning style of your supervisee fit with the dominant styles and culture of the organisation?

The impact of organisational structures and cultures

One part of the supervisory role entails 'helicoptering' above the details of a situation to look for patterns of behaviour or organisational structure that can compromise the work. Organisations have very different cultures and expectations of staff. The National Health Service generally has a 'sink or swim' culture within a strictly hierarchical structure. State schools are greatly driven by the imperatives of the inspectorate. Businesses may have a demanding focus on profitability. The cultural context can directly influence your early meetings with a supervisee. An external supervisor in a hospice worked with junior doctors and always began by asking what the word 'supervision' meant to them; they almost invariably answered 'being told off'. The initial contracting then became a discussion about working together on what they needed to learn, and how to take better care of themselves in order to do their work.

> *Reflection point*
> How well do you understand the vision of the organisation and its operational policies? How do the organisation's roles fit together, and who are the informally influential people? How efficient is the allocation of work or referrals to your supervisees so that they get people they are capable of working with effectively in the time allowed?

In many organisations, workers feel shamed by hierarchical management styles and cultures, and at risk of exposure and humiliation if they fail to deliver to organisational standards. The supervisor's task is to work as an ally with supervisees in such environments, to create a safe place where everyday mistakes can be explored rigorously to improve future practice. You might say to such supervisees: 'I will always inform you of any concerns I might have about your work before I speak to anyone else, and I will ask you to tell me from your point of view what happened. Tell me now, before this happens, are there any things I could do that might make it easier for you when we have to talk about such matters?' Common responses are 'Just spit it out' or 'Give it to me straight' (or words to that effect). At the same time it is respectful to ask your supervisees to let you know if you inadvertently upset them. The power differentials might mean they are hesitant to do that until the relationship is well established.

The value of supervision

Supervision is a precious space where the supervisee can let off steam about matters that upset them: a bullying manager, an incompetent colleague, service users who are frightening or disturbing. Then you have to agree if any action is required, and what support the supervisee might need from you to take it.

In hard times created by the culture, society, economic crises or external systems in which we work, we have to ask ourselves: 'How far can I change the system I am experiencing as stressful, or change myself?' or 'What will it cost me to continue as I am in the hope of living with it?' or 'Should I leave?' Setting realistic goals and identifying who will support the supervisee is crucial. Sharing decision making, agreeing on common objectives with co-workers and creating a culture of mutual respect where 'the other' doesn't have to be wrong just because they are different lays the basis for a balanced working team. This *can* happen in some settings, and it takes careful work.

You and your supervisee each need to have your ethical framework to hand when you meet, so you can refer to it to aid your decision making about tricky situations. This is particularly crucial when you are working to different frameworks. It may help you both when addressing issues of equality and difference, and when the supervisee is a trainee it helps them to learn how to think about core imperatives of good practice. Several authors in Wheeler and King (2001) explore the dilemmas of supervisory responsibility in relation to supervisees.

Most organisations now have staff born in many other countries, so issues of language, assumptions, difference and equality in relation to transcultural misunderstandings can be frequent. Encouraging workers to be interested in difference and how to explore it may create a base for a safe supervisory alliance with you, and improved relationships between colleagues.

If you are an external supervisor to the organisation, do not forget the nuts and bolts of supervision:

- Who will pay you? Do you have to send an invoice?

- What happens if you are ill; do you contact supervisees or does the organisation?

- What feedback is expected and how is it managed?

- What are the confidentiality arrangements if you are supervising a trainee who needs to make recordings of their work for their training?

- To whom do your notes and the notes of the worker belong, and how and where are they to be kept?

Recommended reading

Carroll, M. and Holloway, E. (1999) *Counselling Supervision in Context*. London: Sage.

> Pages 153-154 list the shifts of focus that supervisors might help counsellors who work in organisations to make, to take account of the context.

Hawkins, P. and Shohet, R. (2012) *Supervision in the Helping Professions* (4th ed.). Maidenhead: Open University Press (McGraw-Hill).

> This book has very useful chapters in the whole of part 4 on the organisational approach.

CHAPTER 13

Exploring Group Supervision

> **Key points**
> - Self-awareness is an important prerequisite when working in groups.
> - There are both advantages and disadvantages to group supervision.
> - Peer group supervision can help to develop your group skills.

Group supervision, where three or more practitioners get together, is very different from working one-to-one and less fully understood. When well facilitated, supervision in a group setting can offer many advantages and rich learning opportunities. On the flip side, there are potential hazards, and handling them requires a sound understanding of group dynamics, and knowledge of skills specific to group facilitation. A complete description of the many key skills and processes involved in group supervision is beyond the scope of this chapter. The focus is more modest: to encourage you to reflect on your past experiences and roles in groups, and, unless you have previous experience, to point you in the direction of some resources to support you to facilitate supervision groups in future. The chapter also provides additional specific focus on setting up peer group supervision.

Your first group

Self-awareness is very important if you are to get the most out of working in a group. One place to start in this self-understanding is to reflect on your very first group experiences. We were all born into some form of group, and as children we needed to create our unique place and way of being amongst our siblings (if any), peers and elders. All of us have a fundamental need to belong to the group (Adler 1992); however, we will also have experienced moments of childhood inferiority and insignificance. So in groups, as well as bringing our positive resources, we may also act out these discouraged aspects of ourselves (see the 'Crucial Cs' model in Chapter 2).

> *Reflection point*
> Think of training or supervision groups in which you have been involved as a member, rather than leader. What specific roles did you take? (e.g. 'responsible one', 'joker', 'challenger', 'the quiet one' etc.). How similar are these roles to those you took as a child in your family and with your siblings or peers?

Considering group supervision

Saving time and money may be a key practical consideration when you are thinking about group supervision, and it could be tempting to rush into organising group sessions before weighing up other pros and cons. Some additional positive reasons include:

- members benefiting from multiple viewpoints and varied feedback

- having a greater opportunity for working with difference and diversity

- experiencing a supportive framework that can also enable team cohesion

- a chance to share intuitive responses and gain an increased understanding of the dynamics between the service users and practitioner (see also Chapter 9).

Identifying potential hazards is also crucial. Examples include:

- having less 'special' time for each supervisee

- boundary issues occurring with group members knowing another member's working context or individual service users

- unspoken negative dynamics being acted out, resulting in an undermining atmosphere between group members that also impacts on the actual professional work.

Reflection point

Think about your own experiences of individual and group supervision. What advantages and disadvantages of each do you identify? What form of supervision do you believe would be most helpful in your working environment?

Types of supervision groups

If you are opting to undertake group supervision, you need to consider what type of group will be most helpful for your work context. Proctor and Inskipp (2008) identify four types as follows:

- *Authoritative.* The supervisor takes responsibility while others observe.

- *Participative.* The supervisor takes responsibility but encourages the rest of the group to participate as co-supervisors.

- *Co-operative.* The supervisor monitors and supports the group in developing their own system of supervision.

- *Peer.* Supervisory responsibility is shared equally amongst peers.

> *Reflection point*
> Reflect on groups in which you have participated or facilitated in relation to these types. What would be your preferred mode and why?

If you are new to facilitating group supervision, participation in a peer group can be an invaluable starting point for development of your group understanding and skills. For this reason, peer group supervision is the main focus of this chapter.

Peer group supervision

A feeling of equality is a crucial aspect of a peer supervision group where colleagues work together without requiring the presence of an identified 'expert' supervisor. It usually involves reciprocal arrangements in which peers share expertise, experience, mutual trust and support. Like all supervision, it has as its aim the three main supervisory tasks: the normative, formative and restorative functions

(Inskipp and Proctor 1988) that come together to enable the development of professional competence. Of course, there can also be a danger of poor boundary maintenance, sloppy professional ethics and tricky personal dynamics. With these challenges in mind, as there is no group leader, there is even more need for a rigorously negotiated working agreement (see Chapter 2).

Setting up a peer supervision group
Group composition
Will this be a group formed of members of your team or colleagues that work with you regularly? Do you want it to be made up of differing disciplines working in one agency, or perhaps the same disciplines working in differing organisations? Will you form a peer group with others who trained with you? Whatever you decide, it is important that members have similar needs, approaches and levels of experience.

Group size and commitment
How many members? From three to six can work well; if there are more, it is unlikely there would be sufficient time to meet each member's needs, and this in turn could compromise the quality of their work. Are all committed and able to attend? To maintain continuity in the development of the group, there needs to be positive commitment rather than 'dutiful' attendance. In many organisations, competing priorities may well impact on attendance, and potential difficulties here need to be discussed at the outset.

Group agreement

In addition to the working agreement issues raised in Chapter 2, the following contractual points are particularly important for peer group supervision (Hawkins and Shohet 2012):

- *Difficulties arising from service user or organisational confidentiality* are a possible issue where members work alongside or live near each other, and dual relationships commonly emerge. Discuss beforehand how you would manage a situation where you might know the client or colleague that another member is bringing. For example, will you leave the room while this individual is being discussed, or will the person presenting need to take it to another supervision forum?

- *Set clear ground rules* about respectful communication and feedback. Openly discuss each member's preferred styles of interaction and expectations of supervision and what will help to make it both safe and also extending for each person. What differences are present and how will they be honoured? How will the sessions be structured in terms of making space for a general group 'check-in' and 'check-out', as well as allocating time for each member's presentation?

- *Address ethical practice.* It can be particularly difficult to challenge a peer group member's poor or unethical practice. Discussing this possibility openly at the outset and deciding together how this would be addressed is crucial.

- *Agree firm boundaries* for sharing time equally to minimise resentments. Also create boundaries around the supervision material for each member's contribution so there is no blurring of content into the next person's presentation or beyond the session. This will help everyone to engage fully knowing their material is safely contained.

- *Clarify the roles of each member of the group.* For example, who will organise the meeting room? Who will keep an eye on time boundaries? Will these roles be shared and exchanged?

- *Arrange review sessions* every few months to check on each member's experience and role in the group. Make a space to develop and review the working agreement as necessary.

Reflection point

Identify any kind of peer group with which you have been involved. How was the working agreement negotiated? What additions to the agreement, if any, could have helped further improve the group process?

Peer supervision group processes

Begin the session with a short 'check-in', with each member stating specifically the supervisory issues they want to bring. This can also be a time to share briefly any personal issues that may be impacting in the immediate moment. This personal sharing, clearly differentiated from therapy, not only provides a space for building group connection, but may also reveal important dynamics occurring in the work of that particular peer member. Once everyone's needs are heard, a mutually agreed and timed-session agenda can be set.

CASE STUDY: SESSION CHECK-IN

In their 'check-in' Tania shared that she was feeling rested after a holiday, having seen two 'easy' clients since the last supervision, and wanting only to review one client's positive progress. Liam stated he had been avoiding getting down to his professional accreditation applications and also he had a particular concern about a patient who was self-harming. He wanted to explore the dynamics going on with this patient, and also to gain some support for his accreditation process. Fatima calmly and 'laughingly' described how she was caring for her elderly father along with a double caseload of clients as her colleague was presently off sick. She stated that she was managing fine, and if Liam wanted more time to discuss his two issues, that was agreeable. Tania and Liam challenged Fatima about this and it was ultimately agreed that Tania would offer some of her 'time' to Fatima. This enabled Fatima to receive some essential supervision on the considerable demands of the past two weeks, and her established habit of not asking for help.

During any group supervision, there are likely to be some complicated and perhaps confusing interactions occurring. In the dual role of supervisor and peer group member, it is even more important to notice how you are responding by taking a 'helicoptering' position, so you can reflect on the dynamics.

Below is an example of 'parallel process' (see Chapter 9), a reflection of the work with a parent being played out in the 'here and now' of the peer group, and how new insights were identified by bringing these dynamics into conscious awareness.

CASE STUDY: PARALLEL PROCESS IN A GROUP

A group of early years managers had been working co-operatively and respectfully for a few sessions in peer supervision. Maria, who was presenting her work with a parent, became uncharacteristically angry, stating that she felt criticised by the others in the group. Her peers expressed their bewilderment, as they felt they had been empathic and respectful. Natalie, observing the process, asked Maria if she felt that her experiences in the group right now had any resonances with the client's mode of behaviour. With sudden recognition, Maria shared the realisation that her experience of being criticised in the group mirrored the parent's own feelings of being criticised by Maria, despite all her efforts to be empathic. The group was then able to support Maria with the real issue of how she might best communicate with the parent in future.

So it is not enough to work cognitively. You need to be open to absorbing visual, auditory and body sensations as a means of monitoring the group dynamics. This involves developing the skills of 'listening' continuously to this external and internal information, and making sensitively paced decisions about when to share these experiences with the group.

Although there are hazards, peer group supervision can provide an excellent foundation for building skills in reflective practice and enable a learning culture in teams and organisations. It can work well both as an addition or alternative to regular supervision, and is particularly useful for supervision of supervision (see Chapter 14). If you are not experienced in group work, it will be enormously helpful to gain experience as a supervisee in a well-led participative supervision group. If this is not available, developing a peer group, alongside studying more about group dynamics, will provide a valuable foundation.

Recommended reading

Houston, G. (1993) *The Red Book of Groups and How to Lead Them Better*. Aylsham: Rochester Foundation.

> This little book is packed with creative guidance about leading all types of groups.

Proctor, B. and Inskipp, F. (2008) 'Creative Group Supervision with Brigid Proctor and Francesca Inskipp' (DVD). Newport: University of Wales.

> This DVD presents a skilfully facilitated supervision group in action, including setting the working agreement and use of creative group processes.

Proctor, B. (2008) *Group Supervision: A Guide to Creative Practice* (2nd ed.). London: Sage.

> This unique book, well illustrated by case studies, covers a vast range of practical and theoretical topics essential to developing effective group supervision in many different settings.

Adair, J. (2007) *Develop Your Leadership Skills*. London: Kogan Page.

Bion, W. (1998) *Experiences in Groups*. London: Tavistock.

> These are two well-known group-process models helpful in further understanding group dynamics.

CHAPTER 14

Supporting Your Development

Key points
- Supervision of supervision (SoS) is essential for novice supervisors and desirable throughout professional life.
- SoS in groups combines clinical governance and legal knowledge with facilitative groupwork skills.
- Ethical dilemmas, boundaries, competence of supervisees and training issues are the most common topics covered in SoS.

We recommend that you join a supervision of supervision (SoS) group or have a regular slot where you can discuss your supervisory work. This is essential if the role of supervisor is new to you, and it will continue to be a rich and delightful space for reflection for the rest of your working life. It is not just for beginners.

A very experienced supervisor, when interviewed, said:

What I don't get enough of in supervision is being challenged. People don't challenge me very much. I don't know if that is something about me. I know I can appear very 'know-it-all'. I'm hungry for challenge. I do get it in the supervision group, there are a couple of people who do and my peer supervisor is very good at it. The relief of it! If someone picks up something I don't know or a blind spot, I don't get defensive. I have a *huge* need to be understood. It just gets me in the belly. And then I can do something about it. There's a strength in not colluding.

Anyone experienced enough to be a supervisor usually knows what to do for the best, but not necessarily, and not always. In people-focused work, it is rare to be completely 'wrong' but useful to review decisions and outcomes with the benefit of hindsight and another's thoughtful attention. The description above illustrates the value of SoS and peer relationships that offer support and challenge within a solid alliance. Acceptance without collusion is a sound basis for personal and professional growth. To invite someone to reconsider something they have done and to do this without creating shame is important for the protection of patients or clients, and for the lifelong learning of the worker. To raise a difficult issue about the person's style, approach or choices, and then trust the person to do something about it, is very different from not raising a tricky issue at all for fear of offending.

A SoS group offers opportunities for creative 'play' and continued learning from listening to intuition and inner promptings from all the senses. Using small objects to represent the family or organisation under discussion permits members to see the issue laid out in a more concrete form. They can then offer their reactions and projections to the person being supervised. It is a space where seeing things differently is really valuable. But sensitivity to the norms of people from different cultural backgrounds is important here. In some cultures and environments, respect for seniors makes collegiality and challenge much less acceptable.

SoS for trainee supervisors

A SoS group during a supervisory training enables mature practitioners to apply theories and models, and to build confidence and competence in their practice. Supervision *with* the group gives novice supervisors an opportunity to practise supervising their peers within a safe environment, where everyone is explicit about where their learning aims are focused.

These SoS groups are a space to develop awareness of self, and in which to practise challenging another member without attacking or shaming. Experiencing challenge as useful, when respectfully done, enables a major shift into a developing sense of supervisory authority. One supervisor-in-training wrote:

> SoS provided an opportunity and a forum to explore, for example, gender issues in supervision. Not only gender but also power. I learned a great deal about taking authority, not something I initially recognised but one that I really profited from exploring. From the SoS, where I explored difficulties I was having with the men in a team of volunteers I supervise, I began to explore this area, motivated by the facilitator's reflection that I could move to a stronger 'co-operative' place if I 'clarified my expectations and gave myself permission to exert my own authority' – something I'm aware that I was avoiding without thinking it through, but holding onto an unhelpful injunction that 'nobody likes a bossy boots'.

(Personal communication)

SoS groups should support continued learning. This book emphasises the importance of the contract, and there are specific contractual extras to consider in a SoS group. A written contract agreed between members reminds everyone of the importance of making and sustaining contracts in all supervisory work. As trust develops in this group, it becomes clearer how a contract operates to promote a culture of safety, establish clear boundaries about confidentiality and create a space to learn through observing others and through participation as a learner; thus, written 'ground rules' allow everyone to be clear from the start about how to contribute as a participant and as a witness or co-supervisor. For example, should SoS members state their supervisees' actual names? These people could be current or future colleagues, so supervisory concerns must be discussed with care and respect for their reputation.

'Good group manners' in SoS are the same as for all supervision groups: sharing time fairly, valuing difference and exploring it with curiosity, offering support and challenging appropriately. These practices all contribute to making the group a trusting space. The considerable benefit of having a group with differing perspectives within it results in many possible responses to chew over, accept or reject; thus, the person taking a turn to be supervised in the group can see themselves and their supervisory relationships through other eyes.

CASE STUDY: SELF-CARE WITHIN SELF-DEVELOPMENT

Sharon, a novice supervisor, discussed a supervisee, who was a trainee on a counselling course, whose mother had died quite early into her course. The trainee needed her placement hours, but it was unclear whether her grief meant it was good for her clients for her to continue. Her course tutor was not telling her to stop. The issues the SoS group identified included how the trainee was caring for herself and how her work with clients was being affected. But the key issue was that Sharon had her own history of major loss, and this had affected her reactions. She came to understand more personally that, to avoid 'burnout', supervisors and therapists need time to deal with any reactions. Sharon said, 'Having received the support I needed, I could pass that on to the supervisee, enabling her to continue in the placement but also to take the break she needed once she had completed the counselling hours required.'

The novice supervisor could also develop the courage to enquire very directly, on behalf of the clients, how the work was going. This is important. The chickens of avoidance can come home to roost – when reports are to be written – if the supervisor has not been direct all along.

Ethical dilemmas are a key area of SoS focus. A supervisor in a peer group wrote:

Contracts, ethics, boundaries, confidentiality and the law: these have been frequent topics of our SoS group, particularly in relation to overlapping boundaries which has been a common thread throughout almost every session. I have learned that confidentiality and boundaries are extremely complex, particularly within a small community; to view each case on its merits and to take particular regard to the ethical imperative of beneficence: whether the interests of the client and the supervisee are sufficiently safeguarded.

(Participant on Diploma in Supervision, Cambridge Supervision Training)

Reflection point

The personal accounts given above highlight the value of SoS, especially for personal development and ethical problem solving. If you have had your own experience of SoS, what have been the benefits and drawbacks for you? What are your thoughts and feelings about creating or joining an SoS group for yourself?

One-to-one SoS

In some organisations and cultures, group SoS is unlikely for financial reasons. One-to-one SoS is then useful, and may be easier to organise for professionals practising in rural areas or for those who have responsibilities that make attendance at a group unlikely out of working hours. In the privacy of a one-to-one supervisory relationship, it is possible to consider more personally your own contribution to any difficulties in relationships with supervisees, your adaptability (see Chapter 3) and the efficacy of your own work, and thereby discover whether you might be doing harm rather than good. Regular reviews with the supervisees and SoS are two main ways to keep an eye on this.

Some organisations put staff in impossible positions because of the pressures of time and the difficulties of freeing up staff to attend when they are needed to provide the service. You might be asked to run a supervision group for colleagues from more than one discipline. It is not unusual to find that the group meets too infrequently, for too short a time, without regular attendance, for people of unequal status and power, and works to differing ethical codes of practice. Yet it may be a requirement of your role that you do this. Consultative supervision of supervision is essential to support you to negotiate with your managers, create a realistic contract and agenda, and to plan regular reviews to discover if it is useful and, if so, why.

Reflection point

What challenges do you anticipate if you are supervising in your place of work? What practicable opportunities are there for a SoS group or one-to-one supervisory support for yourself?

Recommended reading

Henderson, P. (2009) *A Different Wisdom: Reflections on Supervision Practice*. London: Karnac Books.

Chapter 18 explores SoS in more detail, describing how it encourages supervisors to stay alert and give time and energy to monitor their practice.

CHAPTER 15

Ending and Moving On

> **Key points**
> - Responses to the ending of a supervisory relationship may touch on past losses.
> - Discussion about ending is an important part of the initial contracting.
> - Giving time in supervision for reflection during ending can enable closure.

Coming to the final pages of this book brings endings in supervision into sharp focus. The conclusion of any relationship triggers varying emotional responses in individuals and teams, often touching on past issues of loss. This may be why purposeful discussion of endings, in both personal and professional relationships, is so frequently avoided, or perhaps briefly touched on only at the end point itself.

There are many types of ending in supervision. Those endings anticipated in advance include time-limited agency arrangements, and when supervisees finish their training or placement or reach a new stage of professional development. Situations not mutually agreed or planned ahead of time may occur when the supervisor or supervisee moves away, becomes very ill or – most unexpectedly – when there is a death. If there is a serious breakdown in the supervisory relationship, or if there seems to be an irreconcilable mismatch between you and your supervisee in terms of your approach, it may be very difficult, or even impossible, to achieve a clear contractual resolution at all. So while it may seem contradictory, discussing endings right at the beginning of your supervisory contracting is a valuable part of providing a safe and sound containment for the work. Here are a few examples of questions that could be used:

> What would be important for you when we begin to plan our ending?

> How often shall we review our time together and agree on our length of contract?

> If our supervisory contract needed to end earlier than planned, what alternatives are available to ensure the well-being of your clients and yourself as a professional?

There are practical administrative actions to take at the end of a supervisory relationship; for example, shredding notes after an appropriate time, or archiving them safely. You might choose to explore what future plans the supervisee may have for supervision. Often there are reports or references to write. Less practically, you may simply want to celebrate if the supervisee has successfully graduated or got a new job.

The process of ending a supervision relationship needs to be given plenty of time and space, especially when there have been previous difficulties or major wobbles in the working alliance. Inviting your supervisees to review what has gone well overall in supervision, and what could have gone better for them, enables a move towards respectful closure. Equally, honouring your supervisee's strengths and development over the period you have worked, while also identifying future learning edges, brings together the past and future. Michael Carroll (1996) captures this eloquently when he states, 'Termination in supervision is a golden chance to anticipate the future by considering the past' (p.114).

This book has aimed to offer a practical guide to support your development as a supervisor. At this ending point we invite you to reflect on your own learning in relation to supervision. What has caught your imagination most vividly? What do you appreciate about your supervisory skills and abilities so far? How might your current supervisor (or a new one!) help you to develop your practical skills and extend your theoretical knowledge further?

We hope this book has given you plenty of ideas to consider as you look ahead. In the meantime, we wish you every success in your ongoing journey as a practical supervisor.

Recommended reading

Copeland, S. (2005) *Counselling Supervision in Organisations: Professional and Ethical Dilemmas Explored.* Hove: Routledge.

> Chapter 11 (pp.172-89), 'Endings and New Beginnings in Supervision', offers a valuable overview of the importance of clear ending processes in supervision, particularly related to organisations.

Henderson, P. (2009) *A Different Wisdom: Reflections on Supervision Practice.* London: Karnac Books.

> Chapter 17 discusses endings and retirement, reviewing the mix of personal and professional issues that endings raise.

Bibliography

Adair, J. (2007) *Develop Your Leadership Skills.* London: Kogan Page.

Ansbacher, H.L. and Ansbacher, R.R. (eds) (1964) *The Individual Psychology of Alfred Alder.* New York: Harper & Row

Adler, A. (1992) *Understanding Human Nature.* Oxford: One World.

Anthony, K. and Nagel, D. M. (2009) *Therapy Online.* London: Sage.

Armstrong, K. and Schnieders, L. H. (2003) 'Video and Telephone Technology in Supervision and Supervision-in-Training.' In S. Goss and K. Anthony (eds) *Technology in Counselling and Psychotherapy: A Practitioner's Guide.* Basingstoke: Palgrave.

Battye, R. and Gilchrist, A. (2009) 'Person-Centred Supervision Training Across Theoretical Orientations.' In P. Henderson (ed.) *Supervisor Training: Issues and Approaches.* London: Karnac Books.

Bettner, B. and Lew, A. (1990) *Raising Kids Who Can.* Newton, MA: Connexions Press.

Bion, W. (1998) *Experiences in Groups.* London: Tavistock.

Bly, R. (1988) *A Little Book on the Human Shadow.* San Francisco, CA: Harper.

Bolton, G. (2001) *Reflective Practice: Writing and Professional Development* (2nd ed.). London: Sage.

Bond, T. and Mitchels, B. (2008) *Confidentiality and Record Keeping in Counselling and Psychotherapy.* London: Sage and BACP.

Brear, P., Dorrian, J. and Luscri, G. (2008) 'Preparing our future counselling professionals: Gatekeeping and the implications for research.' *Counselling and Psychotherapy Research 8,* 2, 93–101.

Burnham, J. (2012) 'Developments in Social GRRAAACCEEESSS: Visible and Invisible, Voiced and Unvoiced.' In B. Krause (ed.) *Mutual Perspectives: Culture & Reflexivity in Systemic Psychotherapy.* London: Karnac Books.

Carroll, M. (1996) *Counselling Supervision: Theory, Skills and Practice.* London: Cassell.

Carroll, M. and Gilbert, M. (2005) *On Being a Supervisee: Creating Learning Partnerships*. London: Vukani.

Carroll, M. and Gilbert, M. (2011) *On Being a Supervisee: Creating Learning Partnerships*. London: Vukani.

Carroll, M. and Holloway, E. (1999) *Counselling Supervision in Context*. London: Sage.

Carroll, M. and Shaw, E. (2012) *Ethical Maturity in the Helping Professions*. London: Jessica Kingsley Publishers.

Copeland, S. (2005) *Counselling Supervision in Organisations: Professional and Ethical Dilemmas Explored*. Hove: Routledge.

Dreikurs, R. (1970) 'The courage to be imperfect.' In Alfred Adler Institute (ed.) *Articles of Supplementary Readings for Parents* (pp.17–25). Chicago, IL: Alfred Adler Institute.

Driscoll, J. (2007) *Practising Clinical Supervision: A Reflective Approach for Healthcare Professionals* (2nd ed.). Oxford: Baillière Tindall.

Edwards, J. K. (2012) *Strengths-Based Supervision in Clinical Practice*. London: Sage.

Egan, G. (2013) *The Skilled Helper* (10th ed.). Pacific Grove, CA: Brooks/Cole.

Freeth, R. (2004) 'A Psychiatrist's Experience of Person-Centred Supervision.' In K. Tudor and M. Worrall *Freedom to Practise*. Ross-on-Wye: PCCS Books.

Hawkins, P. and Shohet, R. (2006) *Supervision in the Helping Professions* (3rd ed.). Maidenhead: Open University Press (McGraw Hill).

Hawkins, P. and Shohet, R. (2012) *Supervision in the Helping Professions* (4th ed.). Maidenhead: Open University Press (McGraw-Hill).

Henderson, P. (2009) *A Different Wisdom: Reflections on Supervision Practice*. London: Karnac Books.

Henderson, P. (ed.) (2009) *Supervisor Training: Issues and Approaches*. London: Karnac Books.

Honey, P. and Mumford, A. (1982) *Manual of Learning Styles*. London: Peter Honey Publications.

Houston, G. (1993) *The Red Book of Groups and How to Lead Them Better*. Aylsham: Rochester Foundation.

Inskipp, F. (1999) 'Training Supervisees to Use Supervision.' In E. Holloway and M. Carroll (eds) *Training Counselling Supervisors*. London: Sage.

Inskipp, F. and Proctor, B. (1988) *Skills for Supervising and Being Supervised*. (Private publication.)

Inskipp, F. and Proctor, B. (1993) *The Art, Craft and Tasks of Counselling Supervision, Part 1: Making the most of Supervision* (1st ed.). Twickenham: Cascade Publications.

Inskipp, F. and Proctor, B. (1995) *The Art, Craft and Tasks of Counselling Supervision, Part 2: Becoming a Supervisor* (1st ed.).Twickenham: Cascade Publications.

Inskipp, F. and Proctor, B. (2001) *The Art, Craft and Tasks of Counselling Supervision, Part 2: Becoming a Supervisor* (2nd ed.). Twickenham: Cascade Publications.

Jenkins, P. (2007) *Counselling, Psychotherapy and the Law*. London: Sage.

Kagan, N. (1980) 'Influencing Human Interaction: Eighteen Years with IPR.' In A. K. Hess (ed.) *Psychotherapy Supervision: Theory, Research and Practice*. New York, NY: Wiley.

Kahn, M. (2001) *Between Therapist and Client*. New York, NY: Owl Books.

Ladany, N., Hill, C. E., Corbett, M. M. and Nutt, E. A. (1996) 'Nature, extent and importance of what psychotherapy trainees do not disclose to their supervisors.' *Journal of Counseling Psychology 43*, 1, 10–24.

Lahad, M. (2000) *Creative Supervision*. London: Jessica Kingsley Publishers.

Lew, A. and Bettner, B. L. (1995) *A Parent's Guide to Understanding and Motivating Children*. Newton Center, MA: Connexions Press.

Millar, A. (2007) 'Encouragement and other Es.' *Therapy Today 18*, 2, 40–42.

Millar A. (2009) 'Developing Skills: Practice, Observation and Feedback.' In P. Henderson (ed.) *Supervisor Training: Issues and Approaches*. London: Karnac Books.

Mitchels, B. and Bond, T. (2008) *Legal Issues Across Counselling and Psychotherapy Settings*. London: Sage and BACP.

North, G. J. (2013) 'Recording supervision: Educational, therapeutic and enhances the supervisory working alliance.' *Counselling and Psychotherapy Research 13*, 1, 61–70.

Page, S. and Woskett, V. (2001) *Supervising the Counsellor: A Cyclical Model.* Hove: Routledge.

Proctor, B. (1997) 'Contracting in Supervision.' In C. Sills (ed.) *Contracts in Counselling.* London: Sage.

Proctor, B. (2008) *Group Supervision: A Guide to Creative Practice* (2nd ed.). London: Sage.

Proctor, B. and Inskipp, F. (2008) 'Creative Group Supervision with Brigid Proctor and Francesca Inskipp' (DVD). Newport: University of Wales.

Proctor, B. and Inskipp, F. (2009) 'Group Supervision.' In J. Scaife (ed.) *Supervision in Clinical Practice* (2nd ed.). Hove: Routledge.

Progoff, I. (1975) *At a Journal Workshop.* New York, NY: Dialogue House Library.

Ronnestad, M. H. and Skovholt, T. (2012) *The Developing Practitioner.* Hove: Routledge.

Scaife, J. (ed.) (2009) *Supervision in Clinical Practice* (2nd ed.). Hove: Routledge.

Scaife, J. (2010) *Supervising the Reflective Practitioner.* Hove: Routledge.

Scanlon, C. and Baillie, A. A. (1994) 'A preparation for practice? Students' experiences of counselling training within departments of higher education.' *Counselling Psychology Quarterly 7*, 4, 407–427.

Schuck, C. and Wood, J. (2011) *Inspiring Creative Supervision.* London: Jessica Kingsley Publishers.

Skovholt, T. M. and Ronnestad, M. H. (1992) *The Evolving Professional Self: Stages and Themes in Therapist and Counsellor Development.* Chichester: Wiley.

Stewart, J. (2002) 'The Container and the Contained: Supervision and the Organisational Context.' In C. Driver and E. Martin (eds) *Supervising Psychotherapy: Psychoanalytic and Psychodynamic Perspectives.* London: Sage.

Stoltenberg, C. and Delworth, U. (1987) *Supervising Counselors and Therapists: A Developmental Approach.* San Francisco, CA: Jossey-Bass.

Sweeney, T.J. (2009) *Adlerian Counseling and Psychotherapy: A Practitioner's Approach* (5th ed.) New York, NY, and Abingdon: Routledge.

West, W. and Clark, V. (2004) 'Learnings from a qualitative study into counselling supervision: Listening to supervisor and supervisee.' *Counselling and Psychotherapy Research 4*, 2, 20–26.

Wheeler, S. and King, D. (eds) (2001) *Supervising Counsellors: Issues of Responsibility.* London: Sage.

Wonnacott, J. (2011) *Mastering Social Work Supervision.* London: Jessica Kingsley Publishers.

Woskett, V. (1999) *The Therapeutic Use of Self: Counselling Practice, Research and Supervision.* London: Routledge.

Index

Made in the USA
Columbia, SC
23 July 2018